DO LESS,
ACHIEVE
MORE

DO LESS, ACHIEVE MORE

Discover the Hidden Power of Giving In

CHIN-NING CHU

ReganBooks
An Imprint of HarperCollinsPublishers

First paperback edition published 2000.

Designed by Sam Potts

Library of Congress Cataloging-in-Publication Data
has been applied for.

ISBN 0-06-098875-4

02 03 04 ❖/RRD 10 9 8 7 6 5 4

CONTENTS

v

THIRD SECRET
DISCOVER THE DIVINE POWER

FOREWORD

In his classic book, *The Road Less Traveled,* M. Scott Peck begins with the declaration, "Life is difficult."

In this destined-to-be-classic book, Chin-Ning Chu makes the case for life being easy.

After reading the wisdom inscribed on the pages that follow, I am certain you will understand the brilliance of *Do Less, Achieve More.* What appears simple is profound. What is most profound is so because of its simplicity. What is simple should be easy to embrace.

Chin-Ning Chu, the global strategist and visionary, is a remarkably insightful individual from very humble origins. She has that rarest of gifts: the ability to explain complex, timeless truths in understandable, meaningful metaphors and illustrations.

She is the only person in the world who could have written this book. It is more a painting than an assembly of words—more an experiential awakening within than advice.

Do Less, Achieve More addresses the very sources of the cultural drought of modern society. We have everything going for us but too little coming together. We seem to have been shoved into a race we didn't choose and whose finish line we can't picture. Most of us have houses, but not the domestic lives we long for. We have photo albums and videotapes of our children, but not the spiritual strength that underpins healthy families. We're extremely busy, sometimes frantically busy, but we don't quite know where we're going. We cope with the urgent, but keep putting off what we sense is truly important. We try to squeeze in lots of fun, sometimes expensive fun, but we're not really happy. Some of us are doing the right things at the wrong time; some are doing the wrong things all the time.

As we enter a new millennium, we must reexamine and reevaluate the way we think, the way we respond to life's daily challenges in what will be a time of even more astonishing change. In this new era, knowledge is the new power; enlightenment and spirituality can become the seeds of harmony and greatness for the human race.

To water the seeds of human greatness, Chin-Ning has summoned the rainmaker, who teaches us how to do less and achieve more.

> —Denis Waitley, president of The Waitley Institute, author of the national best-sellers *Seeds of Greatness* and *Empires of the Mind*.

THE RAINMAKER

Carl Jung, Sigmund Freud's premier student in the field of psychoanalysis, often spoke of the power of miracles by telling the following story:

There was a village that had been experiencing drought for five consecutive years. Many famous Rainmakers had been called, but they had all failed to make rain. In the villagers' last attempt, they called upon a renowned Rainmaker from afar. When he arrived in the village, he set up his tent and disappeared inside it for four days. On the fifth day, the rain started to fall and quenched the thirst of the parched earth. The people of the village asked the Rainmaker how he had accomplished such a miracle.

The Rainmaker replied, "I have done nothing."

Astounded at his explanation, the villagers said, "How can that be? After you came, four days later the rain started."

The Rainmaker explained, "When I arrived, the first thing I noticed was that everything in your village was out of harmony with heaven. So I spent four days putting myself into harmony with the Divine. Then the rains came."

TIRED OF CHASING

Life was meant to be easy—as easy as it was for the Rainmaker to bring rain. Somehow, through the chaos of chasing after our heart's desires, we have made life difficult.

In this book, you and I will take an in-depth look at how exactly this Rainmaker acquired his superior power of making rain without effort. By understanding the state of our Rainmaker, we can translate the secrets that helped him make rain into bringing us the desired results in our own daily encounters. Before we begin our investigation, let us soberly acknowledge where we are at this moment in our lives.

Many people have confided in me, "I am so tired of struggling and fighting life's battles on every front in an exhausting attempt to get ahead." Even those who achieve material prosperity are beset by the feeling "I can't take it anymore," which mars the enjoyment of the fruits of their labor.

We often spend so much time working, our minds get agitated, our hearts grow uninspired, and our bodies become weary. Everyone seems to be doing more, and despite their best efforts, there is always more to do. The more money that is made, the more that is needed. Even if we grow wealthy and prosperous, we find that there are always new frontiers waiting to be conquered. The vicious cycle goes on. How much stress can one's nerves endure?

Meanwhile, for those who bravely keep their thoughts to themselves, it is easy to see in their eyes, their voice, their body language, and every aspect of their being the same story: "I am tired of chasing; yet, I am caught in a no-win, no-way-out situation. If I don't keep moving faster, the people coming up from behind will trample me. If I don't like where I am right now, how will I like it even lower on the social pyramid? I must pick myself up each day and fight another agonizing, vicious battle." So many have fought bravely, with a lack of joy and an absence of fun in their pursuit of "success."

The solution to this crisis seems to dictate that you give up life, become a hermit, retreat from the world, and live in simplicity with nature. For a small handful, this might be a viable solution. But most of us can't just give up on life because we aren't winning. As a great nineteenth-century Asian master said of one attempting to leave the world after he had failed to manifest his life's dreams, "He did not renounce the world; the world renounced him."

Whether you are chasing success, sustaining your hard-won achievement, or preventing failure, it is often all very stressful. As you reach out to force events and outcomes to bend in your favor, you experience anxiety. When things are not going your way, it's as if your life has an uncooperative will of its own.

RELEASING FROM EFFORT

All of my life I wanted to be a great singer. I have spent more money on voice lessons than anything else. Eventually, I realized the main reason I was not the singer I wanted to be was that my desire to sing well was so strong that it had caused my mind to hold my voice hostage. When I sang, instead of just letting my voice go and simply singing, my mind would try to help my voice to sing. I recognized that, in fact, my voice always knew within itself how to sing. It was my mind that did not know how to sing.

As I released my mind from the effort of trying to sing, my voice was freed instantly. I came to see that the transformation of *any* aspect of our lives can be accomplished beyond the constraints of time and effort. This awesome power resides like a seed held within us in much the same way that a seed holds within itself, and ultimately releases, its hidden power of life to become a bountiful tree.

What I discovered about why I couldn't sing provided me with the insight that life was meant to be as easy as singing. Somehow, along the way of our growing up and growing older, we got all twisted up thinking the way to be successful is to put forth a tremendous effort attempting to bend events to the ways we have envisioned. The result is that life often doesn't submit to our efforts; rather, we bend ourselves out of shape, stressed out and burned out. However, when we release from effort, we allow into our lives the power of miracles.

Helen owned an executive employment agency. In the first two weeks after she opened shop, she placed three separate one-inch-long ads in the *Los Angeles Times* Sunday edition in search of three executives for three separate multinational companies. In two days, the three one-inch ads brought her three perfect executive candidates, and she quickly sealed the deals. Ironically, her three client companies had also placed three separate large display ads in the same Sunday paper, one ad covering more than a quarter page. Yet, the three qualified candidates answered only her one-inch ads.

Miraculous results happen much more often than we are willing to acknowledge. This miraculous and simple power exists limitlessly within the laws of nature, totally free, waiting only to be induced. If we were able to call upon the miracle-creating power at any moment we desired, wouldn't our lives become like sleek vessels sailing on a soft, breezy ocean? To illustrate with Helen's case: Placing the ads was her action-oriented activity; getting the miraculous results was due to the power of her mind and her spirit.

CONCLUSION

What the Rainmaker did was nothing short of creating a miracle. Although miracles are beyond reason and manipulation, you will find that they can be induced by creating an environment within yourself that attracts the elements of synchronicity and hidden coherence. In our everyday lives, we normally don't call them miracles because the word "miracles" sounds too melodramatic. When things mysteriously turn out in our favor, we try to underplay them; we call them good luck. Yet so much of this "good luck" is nothing short of miraculous.

Is there a formula to cause miracles and good luck to happen on command? Our challenge is to discover what constitutes favorable factors that create the results we desire. In other words, if we can increase our odds in generating beneficial results in our lives and work, we will achieve effortlessly, as did the Rainmaker.

FIRST SECRET

FINE-TUNE YOUR ACTIONS

DO LESS, ACHIEVE MORE

When the Rainmaker first arrived in the village, the drought was severe and disastrous. If he were like you and me, he would get very busy very quickly: talking to the villagers about the history of rain patterns and setting up a ceremony hall to pray for rain—but he didn't busy himself at all.

The Chinese word for "busy" consists of two parts. One part symbolizes the human heart, the other part symbolizes death. The meaning that can be extrapolated is that when one is excessively busy, his heart is dead. Yet in our society today everyone praises the virtue of busyness. When people ask you, "Are you busy?" you are most likely to answer, "Yes, I am *so* very busy; I have no time to chat." You will never say, "No, I have nothing to do," even if it is true. We associate busyness with success; only not-so-successful people are not busy. In reality, we find there are plenty of people who are very busy but going nowhere. "Busy" is not always a virtue; it often means the heart is being neglected.

Our Rainmaker's objective is to make rain, not to put on a show. He does not need to feign being industrious to impress anyone. In order to bring about his desired result, he does very little—he settles himself down in a tent and glides into meditation. By doing very little, by embracing ease, he brings a state of harmony unto himself, and from him it overflows into the whole village. By doing less, the Rainmaker achieves more.

One of the main principles taught in *hatha yoga,* the Indian system of physical postures, is to allow the body to relax into a given yoga stretch instead of pushing the body into the desired posture. When you are anxious to get into the full extension and you coerce your body into position, your body inevitably resists.

When you are open and relaxed, working without effort, not attempting to get anywhere, the body opens from inside naturally and allows you to ease into deep and complete stretching. Our attitudes toward success and the obtaining of the symbols of achievement work much the same way.

THE DILEMMA OF ACTION AND ANXIETY

When you are pursuing any task with great anxiety, it takes a tremendous effort to realize a meager result. You are desiring and thinking so much; you are tired even before you start to work. Though your body has performed no task, your mind has been working hard at fighting and resisting your perceived circumstances.

Prior to moving a single muscle, the mind has traveled high and low, through glory and defeat. So much energy is expended within the mind before you have had the chance to engage it in the valid pursuit of your goals that the anxiety of wanting has driven you ever further from achieving what you want. You become as ineffective as a wound-up mechanical doll, spinning involuntarily. You want to be relaxed but don't know how to let go of the thousand details that should have been done *yesterday*. When you force yourself to slow down, you feel guilty.

THE RHYTHM OF EASE AND EFFORT

We think that making an effort is the opposite of being at ease. The paradoxical truth is that effort and ease are not in opposition—they complement each other. Like an Olympic runner, to win a competition you must put forth much effort. Yet in order to ensure maximum performance, you must strike a balance between the effort of striving and the ease of fluid action. The same holds true for figure skating. When skaters put forth too much energy, they overspin and fall. On the other hand, if they don't give their optimal mental and physical effort, they will fall short of their best performance.

The goal to seek in the expending of effort is to have it become effortless. As a ballerina dances on her toes, her beauty and grace show through because of the endless hours of practice she puts in. Luciano Pavarotti has trained himself to sing an entire opera with his voice totally relaxed. In order to have this relaxed voice, he had to train every part of his body to handle the exertion that allows his voice to be relaxed. You have to become strong in order to relax and surrender to life's challenges. Grace and relaxation are supported by great strength. This secret of success that guides the mastery of a world-class singer, runner, or dancer stems from the same principles that lead to a superior person in any endeavor.

THE HARMONY OF COMPROMISE AND STRIVING

Within the dualistic nature of achieving is the power of compromise and striving. Think of how a river embodies these two natures. It compromises with the geographical terrain, eroding and smoothing the way as it goes while relentlessly flowing forward, striving to achieve its ultimate purpose of uniting with the ocean. These two natures are always simultaneously in balance.

The river prioritizes its effort: Gushing on to the ocean is its first goal, and removing or getting around the rock is its second. While achieving its second objective, it never loses sight of its first objective. The river has no time to stop flowing and focus on destroying a single obstructing rock before pressing onward.

In this same manner, while you put forth your exertions in striving to accomplish, remain ever diligent with a watchful eye, seeking out the rhythm of ease on the way to your goal. This principle runs throughout every aspect of our lives. In our marital lives, the first objective is to strive for sustaining and creating a loving and harmonious environment for our family. The secondary objective is to not lose our individuality. In order to strive for our first objective, we often compromise our individual differences.

The same situation can occur in a business negotiation. The primary objective might be to create a cooperative partnership to enhance our company's global market, while the secondary objective is to fight for the best deal possible. In order to achieve the big picture—making the deal—a negotiator needs to balance between making the deal and the necessity to compromise. For without compromise, there will be no deal.

LESS IS MORE

Doing less does not mean doing nothing. Following are some key examples that illustrate how the principle *less is more* can work through every aspect of your life.

1
LET THE WATER BOIL

In order to boil water, you pour it into a kettle and place the kettle over a fire. These actions all involve expending energy. When you close the lid of the kettle, you *let* the water boil. If you become too anxious about the result and keep opening the lid, you hinder the process of heating up the water, and you delay its boiling.

For the entrepreneur or salesman, we are all told that we need to diligently follow up in order to close the sale. Even such a simple concept as "following up" has its delicate nuances and insights. Some salespersons, having found a friendly, potential client, start to follow up in an annoying "air raid" style. They are desperate in wanting to see the deal close, much as the housewife who keeps opening the lid of the pot, wishing to see the water boil really fast. The more desperate he is, the more likely he will lose the deal.

2
KNOW WHAT TO GIVE UP

Focus your resources; know what to give up and what to pursue. I observed a small European publisher who had been scraping by for a long time. Last year, his company published a book that hit the all-time best-seller list. Because of this unexpected success, he had many prestigious authors approach him for publication of their new books.

This publisher wanted to capitalize on his momentum and get out the new books as soon as possible. However, his company did not have the resources to properly publish them. In order to accomplish the task, he had to quickly hire more editors and support personnel, most of whom were inexperienced and not up to the Herculean job. The publisher drove all of his employees into a state of physical and emotional fatigue, with the inevitable result that the work was not carefully supervised.

The books were rushed onto the market, and the quality was an embarrassment to both the publisher and the authors. Furthermore, to fund his expansion, the publisher had exhausted the cash flow created from the original hit book. This led to his premier author suing him for withholding royalty payments. He had bitten off more than he could swallow and ended up with no subsequent hit books and a large financial loss.

Like this publisher, many of us go through a hard

learning curve. We are sometimes motivated by fear and greed and spread ourselves too thin, bending our standards "just a little." Yet, as we look back, the results are rarely satisfactory.

When we have lived long enough, watched ourselves carefully enough, and learned from our mistakes, eventually we stop panicking and chasing after every "good" opportunity.

A while ago, I received a phone call from a businessman in Singapore. He asked me to go to Beijing to discuss an upcoming international technology-transfer conference. He had arranged for me to meet with Li Peng, the premier of China at the time, and Zhu Rong Ji, the mastermind of modern Chinese economic development and the present premier.

The Singaporean told me that he had been promoting me to these top Chinese officials and that I would be the ideal person to headline at this event. The conflict was that I had already made a commitment to appear at the Southern Book Fair in Nashville, Tennessee. The Southern Book Fair was not a big event on a national scale, and I was not the only author scheduled to appear there. I could have canceled the appearance, since it had been set up six months in advance, but I did not feel that would be right. I chose to pass on meeting the top officials in China.

My decision not to meet Li Peng was not based only on the fact that the trade show's brochure had been printed with my name on it, or that the conference organizer would have been disappointed by my absence. It was based on my knowledge that if I am destined to be a great name in my field of discipline, it would happen no matter what the circumstances. Meeting Li Peng would not make it happen. He receives thousands of "faceless" guests every year; I would be just another body parading before him. One meeting would not give me the privilege of picking up a phone and calling him for a favor. But I would have definitely generated stress and chaos for myself and others by changing my committed schedule.

After many years of trying too hard, now I approach my own destiny calmly, knowing what to give up.

3

LET THE ANGEL OF GOOD
FORTUNE CATCH UP

There are some who may work harder than others, but when the Angel of Good Fortune comes to visit, she seems to pass over them.

Richard is a self-employed entrepreneur. He is energetic, aggressive, and smart. However, for a long time, he was not very successful. It was not because he hadn't tried but rather because he tried too hard and too much. Those projects he suspected had a handsome monetary reward he pursued with the intensity of a bulldog grasping a bone. Richard suffocated the deals to death.

When he went on a sales call, he didn't stop selling even after the buyer had decided to buy. The buyer may have felt complete with Richard's presentation, but Richard did not experience that completion. It had been too easy for him, so he felt he had to say more. After that, he still felt incomplete and would say just a little more—until he annoyed the buyer, talked himself out of the deal, and was shown the door.

I chanced to run into Richard a few months ago. When he told me of his recent successes, I asked him what had changed in his life. He replied, "I have learned to control my urge to overdo and sabotage myself. I have stopped frantically running after success. I slowed down my pace and let the Angel of Good Fortune catch up with me." Like Richard, many of us are aimlessly moving forward, frantically chasing after elusive success, unaware that we have passed our destination.

4

USE THE MAGNETIC POWER
OF CONTENTMENT

Contentment seems an elusive goal that goes against our modern culture. In our minds, we all believe that in order to be contented everything in our lives must be going very well. The problem is: What does "going very well" mean if you don't have a contented mind? A discontented mind experiences everything as not good enough. If your business is doing well, others are doing better. If your house is nice, another's house is bigger and better. If your children are smart, the neighbor's kids are geniuses.

The word *contentment* often implies desirelessness and inactivity. It seems to contradict the state needed for aspiring to success. When you are seeking the consummation of a given goal or object, you are presumably in a state of longing or incompleteness—a state of noncontentment that drives you into endless activity. CEOs are never contented with the bottom line, negotiators are never quite satisfied with the deals made, an employee's performance always leaves plenty of room to be improved, a spouse is always wishing his or her other half would be more considerate. Contentment *seems* the last thing on anyone's mind. Outwardly, a successful person appears never contented but fueled by the power of discontent. However, this seeming state of affairs is not the case.

The truly successful person knows the magnetic power of contentment. In order to get better, you must accept whatever positive results you have achieved—even though they may be considered meager—because, wherever you are, that is your only starting point. Contentment is not about beating yourself and others up unnecessarily to achieve even more; nor is it about being satisfied with mediocrity.

Contentment is about taking delight in our positive results while, with gratitude and zest, we challenge ourselves and others in pursuing higher and loftier standards in every aspect of our lives. The power of contentment gives birth to self-acceptance and selfless love. This love then radiates to everything you touch—your work, your family—allowing a space for improvement.

When you work in contentment, each day will bring with it a new perspective on how to approach your projects. When you are open, you will experience the joy of performing your work "in the moment." The worker and the joy of working create a dynamic synergy that, over the span of time, can bring results beyond our wildest expectations. How can one achieve this attitude of contentment? The way is to feel contented at all times, even when you feel that you are momentarily discontented.

CONCLUSION

The Angel of Success is a demanding mistress. She wants you to pursue her, and yet she will surely elude you if you strive too hard. In order to capture her, you need to incorporate an atmosphere of ease. By balancing your rhythm of ease and effort, harmonizing compromise and striving, and incorporating the principle of less is more, you will naturally fine-tune your daily activities—from being driven by anxiety to calmly striving in success.

MAKE PEACE
WITH TIME

The subject of *Do Less, Achieve More* would not be complete without speaking of making peace with time. When our Rainmaker arrived at the village, he spent four days in his tent waiting patiently for the moment when heaven would shower its nectar of rain. He set no deadlines as to when the rain was to fall. He took all of the time needed to bring forth an enormous amount of harmony into himself so it could overflow and saturate the whole village. It took him four days to get the job done. When he started the job, the Rainmaker had no idea how long it would take. There was no mathematical formula that he could use in calculating when the village had enough harmony so the rain could fall. He focused on the job rather than on time.

THE DILEMMA OF TIME

Time existed before you and me, and it will be here after we have vanished. Still, to me, time exists only because I exist. Without me, there would be no time. Because I exist, time is here to do battle with me. Time is too short, too long, too boring, too hectic; time flies, time drags; we are late, we are early; we try to buy time, we waste time. We try to manage and control time, but, more often than not, time is in control of us.

Instead of mastering time, we are often mastered by it. We are late for appointments; we are behind in our work; we give up sleep in order to have more time to finish our tasks. We rush here, we rush there, going everywhere, getting nowhere.

Out of desperation, we create the concept of "time management." Time management may not work, but as long as we feel we are doing something to manage it, we feel better about ourselves. As far as time is concerned, time never entered into this agreement to be under our management.

THE TIME MANAGEMENT GURU HAS NO TIME

A production company executive told me an interesting story:

Once they were producing a tape set with Mr. X, who is considered *the* guru on the topic of time management. The production company called Mr. X to check if he had rehearsed the script so they could schedule a recording date. Each time they called, Mr. X always gave the same answer. "I haven't had time to read it."

TIME— THE UNMANAGEABLE MASTER

Mr. X is right, he has no time. In fact his theory of time management, which he had marketed so well, is an illusion. Consider this: Time has existed as long as creation has existed—billions of years. Time is the witness of history and prehistory, and before the concept of history even existed, time was there. How can Mr. X, a speck of dust in the vast expanse of the universe with a life span of less than one hundred years, have any power to "manage" time? At best, we come to realize that "time management" is about managing ourselves, not time. This is the secret that our Rainmaker possessed.

Throughout the ages, mankind has invented instruments—from the hourglass and sundial to the atomic clock—in an attempt to measure, feel, and see time. While humans are busily at war trying to get a grip on time, time stands and ticks away calmly.

An ancient legend tells of an angel in heaven who performed a great ritual sacrifice to the Creator of the Universe. His worship so moved the Creator that He told the angel he could ask for one boon or wish. The angel asked for immortality. The Creator looked troubled. He told the angel this was the one thing that He, the Creator, was unable to grant. "All things," He stated, "will be dissolved in time, even humanity's ideas of God and Creation."

THE CHARACTERISTICS
OF TIME

Let us consider time—its attributes and aspects. However, bear in mind that this is like trying to bottle the ocean in a single container. Since we know that we cannot bottle time's whole ocean, maybe we can find some key characteristics of time that will allow us to peek into its mystery. Once we know something about time, the question becomes: How can we translate these philosophical, conceptual understandings of time into something useful that will make time our supporter instead of our enemy?

Contemplate and meditate on the hidden meanings of the following points until you can experience them as living realities. You will thereby come to inexorably know that you are the embodiment of time, even as you are a player in the midst of the chaos of daily activities.

- The reality of time exists only within us.
- The experience of the length of time shifts according to our state of consciousness. Five minutes may seem to be forever,

and five hours may seem to be a fleeting moment.

- Although time consists of a past and present, with a potential for future, time only truly exists in the moment of "now."
- Time is an infinite series of "nows" strung together.
- Each moment, each "now," carries the entire past and determines the entire future.
- The way we spend each "now" creates our destiny.
- Managing time is about managing ourselves. It is about focus, purpose, and priority. When we are in the moment of "now," we are in timelessness—the eternity, the time beyond time.
- When you live your life by reacting to the outer chaos, you are at the mercy of time, and time victimizes you.
- When you operate your life from the serene stillness of your inner peace, time protects you and serves you.
- When our time is up, no amount of money can buy us a single extra moment.

- If our successes do not become reality before our death, we have only ourselves to blame—we have misused time, our moments of "now."

MANAGE YOURSELF IN RELATIONSHIP TO TIME

Years ago, there was a project that I had procrastinated on for over fourteen months. Finally I had no more time to hide and had to face it. Miraculously, through my subjective measurement of the amount of work I was accomplishing, it felt like hours had flown by. When I raised my head to look at the clock, I found only five minutes had passed. Since this happened repeatedly, I thought my clock was broken and got up to check my living-room clock—the time was the same. I still could not believe it and found my watch in my purse to make sure all the clocks were correct. This task had caused me agony for over a year. It took me a total of three hours to finish it.

While I was doing the work, time seemed to just stand still and stare at me.

Out of this experience, I realized time is not fleeting. Even five minutes is a *long* time. It is human ignorance that does not recognize that time is always full of abundance and potentiality. However, because I experienced the elasticity of time fully in that single incident, it was enough to bring me to the understanding that I could never lie about not having enough time ever again. I could never again say that twenty-four hours does not provide enough time in a day. Now, when I don't have enough time to finish my work, I know the problem is not time; it is me.

The following tips can provide you with another angle to look at how to manage yourself in relationship to fine-tuning your utilization of time:

1

GET TO KNOW
YOUR OWN CHARACTERISTICS

How you use your time has everything to do with your personal character traits.

If you are indecisive, foggy-headed, aimless, unclear about your objectives, you may find yourself very busy, working long hours, and yet accomplishing very little. If you are a deep thinker, you can find that you are very inefficient, ineffective, and irritable when you have to do multiple tedious tasks. However, you can create masterful work when you are assigned an extensive task that involves deep concentration. In this situation, time can stand still for you.

If you are action-oriented and physical you will function better with multiple tasks requiring less thinking and more motion. You will find yourself drawn to tasks that allow you to manifest your goals in the real world.

2

ASSIGN THE WORK

After understanding what kind of tasks are best suited for you, get help for or assign the work that you don't do well to others. If you are not in a position to give those tasks away, challenge yourself to find the lesson that is there for you to learn in that work. Remember, with the proper attitude, you can do anything well.

3

WHEN YOU ARE FOCUSED,
TIME IS YOUR PARTNER

The common complaint of having no time often comes from allowing everyone around you to steal your time. At work, colleagues stop by your desk to make small talk, unexpected phone calls occur, visitors drop in. It seems that uncontrollable elements steal your time and make you the victim. The truth is, when you are out of focus first, you subconsciously permit these disturbances. I have watched this principle at work over and over again in my own life.

When I am deeply into writing a book, the Universal Intelligence makes sure I am not terribly disturbed; if the phone rings, I may not answer it so that I do not lose my train of thought. Even if I do answer the phone, the party on the other end (if he or she has any sensitivity at all) can immediately detect that I am deeply involved and will make it short. Otherwise, I will tell the caller to cut it short or to call back at a better time.

The same thing occurs when I am totally focused on mastering tasks; I also do not idle my time away. Even unexpected visitors or telephone calls do not

26

become obstacles. From my voice they know that I do not wish to be disturbed. Conversely, when I am totally on purpose, I find that I often attract the specific, beneficial phone calls that tend to help me expedite the completion of my immediate tasks. No joke, it works every time.

4

STATE YOUR PRIORITIES

How does one sort out their priorities and decide how to rank them properly? Nikki Rocco, the president of Universal Pictures Distribution, may have the best definition for maximizing this process in the workplace. She said, "Every day I ask myself, 'What is most important to my division and to the people I report to?' Then I put my priorities in order." This way, you can be certain you are taking care of business and not just spinning your wheels.

5

BE A DETECTIVE

Investigate exactly how you end up frittering your time away. While you do your daily chores, half of your mind should be engaged in performing the work while the other half watches how the time ticks away. Become aware of how much time has evaporated. You might discover that it is not so much that you do not have enough time; rather, it is that you are working without direction instead of charging ahead to complete your task. You move the work from the left side of the desk to the right side of the desk; you are busy but ineffective.

6
LET YOUR DREAM STATE
DO YOUR WORK FOR YOU

Before retiring for bed, go through your daily task list: what you have accomplished and what will be your priority for tomorrow. While you are sleeping, your subconscious mind will begin to seek the means of accomplishing tomorrow's tasks.

This is not done with any effort that disturbs your sleep. It is an automatic, natural programming. Once your mind receives the direction for tomorrow's purpose, it will simmer and get acquainted with the tasks. By the time morning comes you will feel that there is a natural familiarity with your "to do" list. You experience being on top of your day instead of being weighted down by your day. When your competitors wake up and begin to work on *their* "to do" list after breakfast, they will already be ten hours behind you.

7
SIMPLIFY YOUR TASKS

When you receive a fax, if the answer is very simple and straightforward, just handwrite your reply on it and send it back instead of typing out a new fax.

I once read a report that stated the use of the computer to write letters and faxes takes much more time than writing handwritten notes. It takes time to close the screen you are working in, locate the right directory and files, create a new file name, and type in the name of the fax's recipient. It is so much faster to just handwrite the note: "No problem. It shall be done as per your instruction," or any other simple message. The next time you want to print a letter, send a handwritten note—it is so much more personal and time-efficient. Similarly, many tasks can be completed more efficiently when simplified.

8

DON'T WASTE OTHERS' TIME

Before you get on the phone, write down the points you want to make and the objectives you want to have accomplished by the time you hang up the phone. If you can finish a phone call in two minutes, do not take twenty minutes to say the same thing. In other words, as you don't let others waste your time, neither should you waste their precious time, on the phone or in face-to-face meetings.

9

BUY MORE TIME

Pay for the most efficient, high-tech tools to accomplish your job. What you are paying for is not new office technology; you are buying yourself more time. Just be sure that you are running your machines and that your machines do not end up running you.

10

PLAN LESS FOR YOUR DAY

Mr. Lin of Taiwan's *Success* magazine, says, "Instead of piling twenty hours of work together into an eight- or ten-hour day, schedule six hours of work so that you can accomplish it superbly in eight hours. In this way, you will allow time for that unexpected interference. Also always remember, because we live in the physical realm, everything takes longer to do than you think."

11
PLAY LONGER HOURS

To me, work is the highest play, so I don't mind playing a little longer. The more I play, the more I earn.

12
DISAPPEAR THE PAPERS

Lawrence T. Wong is the president of the Hong Kong Jockey Club (Hong Kong's largest taxpayer) and the past president of the Ford Motor Company of Taiwan, the most profitable foreign venture in Taiwan. While I was visiting his office, I found his office had not a single piece of paper laying about. I asked him how he did it. He stated, "You should never touch the same paper twice. Once you have touched it, there are three things you must do with a given piece of paper: handle it, file it, or throw it away."

For those papers that are just screaming "keep me, keep me" and don't want to be thrown away, Larry Wong also has a method:

1. Create three drawers: A, B, C
   A—Relatively important
   B—Less important
   C—Least important
2. Every 7–10 days, throw away all the paper in Drawer C.
3. Then, demote Drawer B to C and Drawer A to B. In time, all the papers will be handled without ever having to handle them.

When I asked how he came up with this method, he told the following story:

He once worked for a boss who kept mountainous piles of paper on his desk. Curious as to what his boss's reaction might be, he hid one pile of his papers in the closet for a month. His boss never missed them. He then brought those papers back and hid another pile. His boss again did not realize anything had changed. His conclusion was that his boss had been using his desk as an archive filing cabinet.

Many of us are also using our desks as storage instead of using the filing cabinet. By doing this we create chaos for our minds. We are sending our mind the subconscious message that we have more to do than we actually do. Our mind becomes agitated by the overwhelming volume of the paper on our desks and, consequently, is not sharp and precisely focused on the immediate task that is before it.

The answer—Clean it up!

13

ANTIDOTE FOR A MILD CASE OF ADD (ATTENTION DEFICIT DISORDER)

Occasional ADD is a common condition to which many of us are prone. It is usually created by interaction with our overly demanding world. For those who have never experienced it, you cannot imagine how irritating it can be when it occurs.

On one occasion, for example, I noticed that I had walked into my bathroom but, upon arriving, had forgotten why I had gone there. I stood in front of the mirror and asked myself, "Why am I here?"

Eventually, I remembered that my original purpose was to wash my face.

To cure this situation, you must mentally verbalize your initial thought (wash face, get coffee, etc.) before and during your excursion. If you have these mild ADD tendencies and don't do this, the chances are good that by the time you get to your destination you will have had at least ten more unconscious thoughts that will have crowded out your original impulse to action.

So, the remedy is to follow this sequence of events:

1. A thought triggers your initial desire for action, such as washing your face.
2. Say it silently or softly to yourself: "washing face."
3. Follow the command by walking to your destination. Verbalize softly your intention while walking to your destination.

If you think this is too much work, compare it to the reward. Practicing this technique will evolve your mind toward being less foggy, becoming more clear with repetition. You will see a dramatic change in your relationship with time. If you ever find your-self saying, "I don't know where the time goes," you are a good candidate for this exercise.

This technique is similar to that which Buddhist monks use to "stay in the present." Whatever action they are performing, they repeat the word as a mental mantra to remind their minds to not drift off in idle rumination. So, while they are walking, they will mentally say "walking, walking"; while eating, they repeat "eating, eating."

14
KEEP YOUR TIME AGREEMENTS
OR RECREATE THEM

You abuse others' time by not being on time, by not keeping your time agreements. It's simple— be a man or woman of your word and think enough of yourself and the other party to keep your time agreements. If the unexpected happens, call the other party to recreate your agreement. Tell them your best estimate of when you can reasonably be there; tell them what is causing your delay so they can choose to wait for you or reschedule.

Many people lie to themselves and say, "I'll be

there in a few minutes and if I stop to call that will just upset them more by pointing out my tardiness." Nothing could be farther from the truth. When you are not on time and you don't call to let the other party know you will be late, you have just told them, "I don't care about you. You have nothing to do except sit and wait for me to show up—whenever I do. I'm too important to be bothered with considering your schedule and that you might have a life!"

Most people will be happy to recreate their agreement with you and set the meeting back thirty minutes or schedule it for another day. It shows courtesy and a recognition that you realize time is important to both of you. The worst aspect of not calling to inform the waiting party of your delay is that, because they don't know whether you will show up in two minutes or two hours, they are placed in a state of time limbo and cannot start a project or handle some business to utilize their time well. When they know that the meeting is set back forty-five minutes, they can then plan what tasks can be accomplished in the allotted time.

It is a strange fact that the most successful people are the most conscious and conscientious about their time and their time agreements. They know that not keeping their agreements causes undue chaos in their lives and everyone else's.

15

PLAN YOUR TIME BACKWARDS

It is much easier planning your time backward rather than projecting forward. Take your deadlines and work them backward, so that you can realistically figure out when you must start your tasks and determine what has to be accomplished by when.

For example, if I'm going to catch a flight departing San Francisco International Airport at 9:00 A.M., then I need to get to the airport at 8:00 A.M. to accomplish all the preliminaries involved. It takes an hour and a half to travel from my home to the airport. Also, I must remember to allow for a possible traffic jam (they happen often), so I need to leave my house two hours before 8:00 A.M. I know it will take me one hour to get ready to leave the house, and, lastly, I add thirty minutes for unexpected problems (missing keys, last-minute phone calls from the East Coast, etc.). This means I must get up no later than 4:30 A.M. to leave the house at 6:00 A.M. to arrive at the airport by 8:00 A.M. in order to catch the 9:00 A.M. flight. No stress; everything is under control.

For twenty years I used to be the Queen of Tardiness—to most of my appointments, I was thirty minutes late. Since I have adopted this backward planning system, I find the most important key is to allow myself more time than needed for that unexpected traffic problem. I learned this from an army general friend of mine. Whenever he has a meeting, he is not one minute late or early—always just on time. Finally I could not stand it anymore; I asked him for his secret.

He told me about his backward planning system as well as always getting to his destination early; even if it means his chauffeur must circle the block a couple of times to make his arrival precise. By "wasting" some of his time, he saves time by never having to deal with the upset and explanations that being late would cause. When you try to plan your time too closely, you may discover that it will cause more time to "fix" it.

16
ALWAYS OVERESTIMATE
THE TIME NEEDED TO
COMPLETE YOUR PROJECT

People tend to underestimate the time needed to complete a task. Years ago, I wanted to build a "romantic" stone house on my Oregon mountain property. I bought a guide book that stated how easy it was to build a stone house with your own, two little hands. In my mind it was a piece of cake. I could just see that little gingerbread house standing in the midst of the green forest. When I started to struggle with the real stones and cement, reality set in.

To get it right, you may want to overestimate your project time by a minimum of three times longer; some projects realistically may take five to ten times longer. This is all according to how realistically you had set your initial estimate. Consider those professional estimators in civil projects, movie budgets, and product development, and how they are almost always into time and cost overruns.

Sean owned a custom software engineering company. In order to sweeten the deal, he often underbid the time for delivery. After the due date came and went, while the software was still in shambles, the client would start to complain. A two-month job would eventually be finished in ten months. During the eight-month schedule extension, he was in hell. All of his energy focused on how to calm the rage-filled client. Often he would have four or five livid clients at the same time.

Eventually Sean lost his business. He had spent so much energy focusing on putting out the fires that it left him with no time to generate new business. Even if he got a potential new client interested in his service, his existing clients would sabotage him by pouring out their upsets when it came time for references.

Sean should have had the courage to estimate realistic times needed to deliver a project. But he was driven by the fear of losing jobs, so he wouldn't tell the truth.

17

FOCUS ON THE JOB,
NOT THE TIME

When a project becomes violently driven by time, stress and fear set in as job integrity goes out the window and disaster strikes. On January 28, 1986, when the Kennedy Space Center launched the tenth space-shuttle flight, it blew up like a giant firecracker on television and killed all eight astronauts on board. My first intuitive thought was that this horrible event had been caused by preventable human error; that someone in charge of the project had been driven by fear of an overrun in the budget or missed deadlines. A year later, the cause of the disaster was disclosed and it proved my instincts to be correct.

NASA had gone ahead though the shuttle was not ready to launch, even though a senior engineer protested that the O-rings had problems. This resulted in the most regrettable and tragic space accident ever. How can you replace the lives of those precious human beings on board? The tragedy was caused by the person in charge having his eyes on the time, not on the job.

18
YOU DON'T HAVE TO DO IT ALL

For the little or the much that you have accomplished today, congratulate yourself. Whatever did not get done, so be it. If you died right now, you would not miss all your unfinished tasks.

CONCLUSION

Understanding time is vital to your objective of do less, achieve more. Without time on your side, there will be no peace of mind or joy in your life. Fine-tune your understanding of time and how you spend it. Take refuge in time: stop managing it, make peace with it. Making peace with time translates into making peace with yourself.

When you are at peace with yourself, then your life, your work, your commitments, your schedules, your "to do" list, and your ambitions will be supported by the synchronicity and hidden coherence of your life that, in turn, gives life to time. For those who are at peace with time—as our Rainmaker is—do less, achieve more is but one of a myriad of rewards in their lives.

TRADE WHAT YOU HAVE FOR WHAT YOU WANT

Faith without works is dead.
> —The Bible, James 2:26

Success is not free—you always have to pay for it with the coin you already have. In order to be a superior Rainmaker, our Rainmaker had to give up being a layabout watching the grass grow or hanging out at the local watering hole getting smashed. In exchange, he had to contemplate and study the mystical elements that create drought and learn how to entice nature's grace to shower forth as rain. It was no small commitment for him to master his professional rainmaking craft.

LIFE IS ALWAYS FULL

Whenever people think of success, they immediately think of "more"—more money, more love, more fun and good times, more respect. Yet, upon examination, success is not about having more. It is about fine-tuning your understanding of what you are willing to give up in order to get what you *really* want.

At any given moment, your life is completely full. Think about it—what was your life like yesterday? You had twenty-four hours, and I guarantee that you used every minute and second of it. You were always doing something—you played, you read, you worked, you fought, you argued, you feared, you worried, you idolized, you breathed, you slept, you ate, you sat, you watched television. Whatever life you had yesterday, it was a full life. You filled every minute of it with something, some activity, even the activity of inactivity.

If you do not like the life that you had yesterday, then you have to not do the same things today that you did yesterday. You have to first give up something from yesterday's list to make room for some new, more exciting, reward-oriented activity.

A CIRCLE FULL OF STUFF

Imagine a circle in space. This circle is filled with "stuff," all the stuff that makes up what you call "your life." This circle of yours contains all the stuff that you call good or bad tendencies and actions. Whether it is filled with more of one type than the other, the circle is always full. In order to add success to our circle of business, relationships, or enjoyment, we have to remove something. We have to give up items we like in order to make room for the good that we really want.

PAY FOR YOUR SUCCESS

In order to have enough energy to sustain your demanding workload, you must exchange the pain of exercise for the fun of a television-watching marathon. You must give up those delicious fatty and sugary foods for that boring, high-fiber, low-fat diet.

In order to improve yourself and get that competitive edge, you have to attend seminars instead of going out with your friends all night to the bars and nightclubs. In order to properly prepare your business proposal and make it a winner, you have to give up your free time on weekends and evenings that you could spend with your family. The list goes on and on.

LIFE IS A SUPERMARKET

Picture your life as a giant supermarket, full of desirable things—material, spiritual, and intellectual. But you cannot purchase anything in this magical supermarket with money. You can only barter with the stuff you already have—your possessions from within your circle.

Try the following mental life-shopping exercise: Go to the market, pick out what you want, and pay for it with what you have. See what you end up with. You should update and reevaluate this list at least once a year throughout your life. Things you thought you truly wanted, you may find you didn't want at all. Things that were not so important suddenly take precedence.

SUCCESS SHOPPING CHECKLIST

LIST 1
SHOPPING LIST:
WHAT DO I WANT?

Divide your life into categories, such as career, relationships, family, health, spiritual needs, pleasure, wisdom, knowledge, or any other topics you consider important. In each category, do deep soul-searching, then write out what you really want to have. The sky is no limit for this list, only your imagination.

Example—Sally's Career: I want to be a supermodel with annual earnings of over a million dollars.

LIST 2
PAYMENT METHOD: HOW TO MANIFEST
MY DESIRES INTO REALITY

The payment method requires taking a sober look at what you have to trade to make room for those new positive results that you want to enter your life. This is a serious how-to process. It is not an unfamiliar process. Each of us goes through this process dozens of times a year when we have to make a decision regarding major purchases.

Consider wanting to buy a Rolls-Royce. That's easy—it only becomes difficult when we have to contemplate how we are going to pay for it. Wanting a Rolls-Royce and determining how to pay for it are two very different things.

Example: From our case above—Sally wanting to be a supermodel—how can she move from the state of wanting to be a supermodel to actually becoming one? What does she have to give up? In other words, how can she pay for her dream profession with the stuff that she already has for barter in her circle?

1. She will trade in her present eating habits, abandoning all the foods she loves in order to lose thirty pounds.
2. She will abandon her couch-potato lifestyle in exchange for working with a fitness trainer four times a week, three hours each day.
3. She will budget her cash in order to pay a physical trainer. That leaves her without spare cash on hand for movies and her regular shopping trips with the girls.

4. She will trade her bingo nights in exchange for dance classes. This means she no longer gets to gossip with her bingo friends about the latest rumors going around the neighborhood.
5. She will shift other spending priorities. Good skin-care products and a stylish haircut and coloring must now take precedence.
6. She will trade her undemanding but secure secretarial job for an endless series of rejections when she goes to cattle calls.
7. She will trade in her tender ego for resilience and courage in order to take the endless rejections that come between the few photo shoots she will be hired for.
8. She will exchange her secure job for a slim chance of maybe or never.

The list goes on. At the end of this effort, Sally will learn where she really stands and what is holding her back from fulfilling her dreams.

LIST 3
CAN I AFFORD IT?
DO I REALLY WANT IT?

In List 3, rate on a scale from 1 to 10 the difficulties you will have to go through to exchange success for your familiar behavior and current way of living. You must ask yourself, "Am I willing to give up my present lifestyle in exchange for having what I really want in business and in life?"

Possibly you will discover that the life you have is exactly the life you absolutely want and that you are unwilling to change a thing about yourself. If so, then you are to be counted among the blessed of humanity. But know this: If you are *not* content, at least you cannot lie anymore about the idea that life has deprived you of your success.

If you are discontented but unwilling to give up what is holding you back, you will have to admit that it is *you* who has chosen to reject success and to abandon the dream of being all of the best you can be. If this is so, you can stop getting jealous whenever you see other people around you succeeding in the life you thought you wanted for yourself.

Remember, you are the captain of your ship. You

always have the choice if you are willing to trade what you already have for what you truly want.

Example: After performing the rating exercise, Sally soberly acknowledged that she did not have what it takes to be a supermodel, nor did she really want to be one if it took all that trouble. Sally had to go back to the drawing board to rethink what exactly she was willing to sacrifice to upgrade her life.

GETTING RID OF
OLD FRIENDS

As you are climbing the ladder of success, you may find yourself naturally moving away from your old, counterproductive companions and friends. As the cream separates from the milk, so your old friends who do not share your commitment to excellence and achievement can exhibit jealousy and envy as you walk out of their lives.

As the old Chinese saying goes, "When you go near red ink, you become red; when you go near black ink, you become black." To know a person's real nature, look at what kind of people he or she spends time with. Nothing influences you more in your lifestyle, success, behavior, or habits than the company you keep. People on their way up commonly find that the first things to fall away from them are their nonsupportive old friends.

Another Chinese aphorism states: "The wise individual's friendship is as light as water. The small-minded person's relationship is as sticky and sweet as honey." A true friend is not one who is in your face constantly demanding your attention. They know your life is not about chitchatting with them; it is about bettering yourself and using your time wisely. In order to be a true friend to you, a person first has to be a true friend to himself. Friends are self-assured and self-supportive; thus, they can support you while not feeling threatened by your success.

On the other hand, the nonsupportive friends are called by the Chinese "wine and meat friends." They love to party with you but burn with jealousy whenever they hear joyous news of your career or personal triumphs.

You may discover that many of these so-called friends are really not friends at all. They hate to see you surpass them. In fact, often those friends whom you consider your really, really, really good friends can be really, really, really jealous of your success. They would much rather see a stranger soar into the sky of accomplishment than to see you flying there. They thought you were one of them, so who do you think you are to be worthy of surpassing them? As long as you are down at their level with them, they will approve of you. Step out with your accomplishments, and you will get scorn heaped upon your head. Because of their inferior judgments of themselves, which keep them bound, they cannot feel happy for you and your advancements. There is nothing you can do to change their minds about you.

You should quietly and graciously walk away. As you clear out your old, jealous companions and useless activities, you are making room for more suitable associations to enter. Let the eagles and dragons enter into your life and begin soaring among the heights and mountain peaks with them. Leave the old rat pack standing on the low plains of mediocrity.

WELCOME GREATER OPPORTUNITIES

Some of the "powerful" people who have previously helped you will also drop out of your life. Do not be devastated by their rejection. You will see that it is the will of the Universe for you to move on to a more beneficial environment where you will expose yourself to greater opportunities.

Have you ever noticed that certain "powerful" people have come into your life at just the right time during different stages of your development? As they have completed their destined journey along your life's path, they naturally drop out to make way for new and more powerful beings to participate with you in making achievements toward your mutual benefit.

ADJUST YOUR ATTITUDE

Tom is a homebody who hates to travel. Ironically, his job requires a great deal of international traveling, as well as sleeping in hotel beds where a thousand strangers have slept before him. Tom hopes that one day the human race will have the technology of instantaneous transportation made famous by the *Star Trek* series—"Beam me up, Scotty"—so that he can go anywhere in the world, take care of business, and return home all within the snap of a finger.

However, since that day may be far off, Tom had to adjust his attitude toward travel. Instead of thinking, as he used to, about how awful it is to travel so much, he now thinks of traveling as downtime he can spend to clear his mind, be alone, and review his business and personal progress. In a strange town and yet another hotel, he finds that this is a good time to catch up on his relaxation by going to a sauna or getting a massage. Now he looks forward to his travel.

Wanting what you don't have or hating what you do have is the fast track to anxiety. Change your mental state from experiencing pain in what you must do and find within it the experience of fun and adventure. Move your attitude from suffering to joy. A whole world of new experiences will open up for you.

PREPARING TO SUCCEED

Before the Angel of Success arrives in your life, you should devote yourself to preparing your welcome for her. Polish your craft and strengthen your body to be fit so that you can do your job and enjoy success when it comes. Sharpen your mind and spirit so that they are ready to face the challenges that accompany a visitation from the Angel of Success.

If you are not ready when the angel knocks, she will flee. And who knows when she will make it back around to your door again? One night in the 1960s, Clint Eastwood and Burt Reynolds were dining together. Clint had already become a famous movie star, but Burt was still struggling, trying to get bit parts. Burt asked Clint what he had done before he got his big break. Clint answered that he had simply "prepared myself for success."

Those unadorned words, *preparing for success,* were the advice that was worth ten thousand ounces of gold to Burt Reynolds. He heard the words, understood the profound principle that they held, and went on to stardom.

CONCLUSION

Trade what doesn't work for what you really want. Often, the greater the reward, the larger the adjustments you will have to make in your life. These may include giving up familiar but counterproductive friends, attitudes, and habits.

For our Rainmaker, on the day he was born he did not come with a letter of introduction from Heaven stating, "He is a great Rainmaker." It was during the course of his life that he became a superior Rainmaker. If our Rainmaker spoke to you now, he would be telling you stories of how he had sacrificed and traded his less productive activities for actions that led him to have a legendary rainmaking career.

ADOPT DIRECTED DREAMING

If you change the contents of your nightly dreams, you can change your life. If your dreams are full of struggle and they overwhelm you, it is most likely that your experience of life is overwhelming. In the same manner, if our Rainmaker's dreams were full of frustration at his inability to bring the nectar of raindrops unto the sun-scorched clay soil, how was he going to manifest rain in the real world? Our Rainmaker, before he could bring rain into the physical world, needed to experience the shower of rain inside himself first.

CHANGE YOUR DREAMS, CHANGE YOUR LIFE

Your dreams are like a movie projector reflecting your conscious and unconscious thoughts. If you want to know the quality of your life, examine the quality of your dreams. You don't have to be a professional dream interpreter; a lot of common sense will do the job.

Gary came from a working-class family. When he was ten years old, during a visit to his grandparents' house with his elder brother, he told his grandparents that when he grew up, he would have a very large mansion. It would be so large they could put their entire house in his living room. His grandparents were amused and said to him, "More power to you." His brother went directly home and told his father what Gary had said. When Gary arrived home he received a terrific beating from his father for being an unrealistic dreamer.

Gary studied hard and became the first in his family to receive a college diploma. After graduation, he worked very hard trying to get ahead in business. By the time he was forty-five years old, due to relocation and job changes, he had bought and sold many residences, but none had ever come near to the grandeur of the mansion he, as a youth, had described to his grandfather. The vision of having that dream house was beginning to look like nothing but an empty boast.

Gary felt frustrated. His small computer business had been growing steadily at 5 percent a year. It was a good business, grossing over a million dollars a year, but not good enough to manifest his dream. His net yearly income was only three hundred thousand dollars. The desire for having his dream mansion was so strong that he had started to dream about houses—beautiful, large houses overlooking the coastline of Miami Beach and houses near New York's Central Park. He even dreamed about a gigantic castle into whose living room he could put his grandfather's house. But in every dream, the houses were not his. They belonged to someone else and he was always trying to figure out how he could purchase the estate for a half million dollars because that was a realistic price he could manage. At the end of his dream, he would have to walk away from his dream home.

Eventually, Gary discovered that there was a pattern to his dreaming. He saw outrageous houses, but at the finish he would always realize that he could not afford them. He felt powerless to obtain any of the magnificent homes. For the opulence level of the house he truly desired, he would need to have a net income of at least three million dollars, and that would be a giant leap from his present reality.

Then a brilliant spark of intuitive insight came to him. He questioned, "I wonder if I could direct my dreams to dream that I *can* afford the house and that I do make three million dollars a year? Can I create in my dream the reality that I already do own my dream house?"

EXERCISES IN DIRECTED DREAMING

Gary started altering his dreams through Directed Dreaming exercises:

1

ADOPT QUANTUM THINKING

Gary was a scientist and, because of that, very realistic. He could not see how he was going to jump from three hundred thousand dollars in net income to three million. He thought about his problem during every hour of the day, while eating, sleeping, or working. There had to be an answer as to how one could jump out of the strictures of reality into the realm of unreality; how one could alter the very fabric of his reality. Being a scientist left him stuck with his worldview steeped in realism. However, being a scientist also provided him with the insight of how the subatomic particles that make up matter leap from one realm to another.

In the quantum theory as articulated by twentieth-century physicists (the most renowned being Niels Bohr of the Copenhagen interpretation) it is stated that an electron inside an atom, under the proper stimulus, disappears from one orbit and then reappears in another orbit. Yet the electron does not travel smoothly from the first position to the other. Effectively, it does not exist in between the two different orbits.

In other words, the electron does not move from one place through space and then land in the new place; it just disappears from one level and instantaneously reappears at another. Gary thought to himself that perhaps within this universe this curious law of physics was not limited to electrons only. Perhaps human beings, also the products of the condensations of matter and energy, would be susceptible to the quantum theory; that if it worked in the electron, it might also be applied to the macroworld of human matters.

He began to observe that events and circumstances in people's lives do not move in linear ways; they also seemed to travel in quantum leaps. He discovered that the strata of wealth and social class existing in the world were akin to the differentiated orbits electrons occupy and that movement between them often came by leaps and bounds rather than in a steady, plodding, predictable fashion. He wondered what force he must apply to bounce his life into the higher, grander orbit.

To effect this quantum leap, Gary decided he should first alter the logical nature of his mind. Within the science of logic existed the mystery of the illogical quantum movement. He saw his logical 5 percent growth pattern was a product born out of his linear-progression-type thinking. A giant quantum leap would have to become the new model for his mind.

Gary realized that his mind was too small to contain the vast, unrealized potential of the universe. He concluded that the author of the universe must be an outrageously big thinker. Gary abandoned his rational mind, his realism, his limitation thinking and embraced wild, unreasonable outrageousness. He saw that the universe as we understand it is infinite in size and that recently science was beginning to speculate that there may exist an infinite number of universes other than the one we know. He saw that placing realistic limitations of thinking on life itself was ultimately unrealistic on our part.

2
LIVING YOUR DREAMS
WHILE AWAKE

Gary discovered that whatever dreams he wished to experience at night, he had to think and live them in that state during his waking hours. He no longer let his dreams dictate their own content. He was going to take an active role in directing the contents of his dreaming. It is a well-known fact that what occupies your thoughts during the day will effect what you dream about at night. Instead of acknowledging

65

the reality of his financial situation, he decided to create his own quantum reality: He would see that he already was earning three million dollars and owned his dream house.

On second thought, he considered, "Why settle for a three-million-dollar house? Why not five million?" And why settle for one house since he could never make up his mind as to whether he wanted his dream house on beachfront property or in the middle of New York City? Why not have multiple dream houses? If the Divine can create an infinite number of universes besides our own, why not dream of earning ten million dollars or more?

Gary engaged the battle between his habitual mind of realism and his newly adopted mind of outrageous quantum thinking. Whether working, playing, or speaking, part of his mind was always watching the other part to make sure that whenever his thoughts fell back into his "real" reality, he would put that old, linear thinking out of his consciousness and reestablish his thought of quantum reality—that he possessed gorgeous houses everywhere, that he made ten million dollars.

At first, this exercise was not easy, but he persisted

in correcting himself. He believed throughout this painful struggle of self-correction that one day, somehow, his old mental patterns would break and just like the electron, out of nowhere, it would collapse to take a quantum leap for the new realm.

3

EMPLOY VISUAL STIMULI

To help him reinforce his new mental images, he added pictures to stimulate his imagination. He cut out colorful, brilliant photographs from magazines that represented his new life in his mind's eye. Upon arising and before retiring, he would study these pictorial stimuli until he felt they were made a part of his life. Whenever he discovered his mind falling back to his old "reality" thinking, he would bring forth the strong photo impressions to erase his familiar reality.

4

EVERY DAY, DO SOMETHING YOU THINK YOU CAN'T

Gary read an exercise in a book about increasing the power and strength of the mind. It stated, "If you have never tied your shoelaces while standing, do that. If you are uncomfortable attending social functions, force yourself to participate in a few with a joyful spirit. It does not matter how insignificant the task may seem, the important thing is that it must be something that you thought you could not do before—or have never tried. Challenge yourself to break through your habitual mental conditioning. Generate at least one such win a day. Sooner or latter, your subconscious mind will register the accumulative effect that being a winner is a daily natural occurrence—your normal state."

Gary started to adopt this simple formula. On the days when he had not accomplished anything in particular for which he experienced being a winner, he ran five miles or did fifty push-ups, since exercise was not one of his strong points. Now, Gary's dreams began to change. He began dreaming he bought a particularly beautiful house in his town's finest neighborhood. This home was, in actuality, owned by an old classmate of his where he had visited on various social occasions. But the twist in his dreams was that he was renting the house to his friend and his old school chum was having difficulty paying the rent. Still, he was making progress in dreamland, for even though he was having his problems collecting the rent, he was now beginning to experience on the mental plane that a grand mansion was actually his.

5

MIMIC THE SPIRIT OF BILLIONAIRES

Gary thought there was definitely a difference between the spirit of a struggling entrepreneur and a prosperous billionaire. He booked a two-week passage on a most exclusive cruise ship, where his fellow passengers consisted of a small elite group of multimillionaires and billionaires. The cost was higher than Gary cared to pay—forty thousand dollars for him and his wife—but he had decided it must be done.

For the two weeks while he was on the ship, he forgot that his "real" financial status was not quite equal to that of his fellow passengers. He felt he was one of them. Gary discovered that the greatest difference between those who lived in twenty-million-dollar houses versus those who lived in houses costing two hundred thousand dollars was the mental boundaries we set for ourselves. A two-hundred-thousand-dollar house is a realistic boundary, a twenty-million-dollar residence is an outrageous boundary.

6
REVIEW YOUR DREAMS
UPON AWAKENING

Upon awakening, while still lying in bed, the first thing Gary would do was close his eyes and review his dreams. If the dreams were positive, filled with confidence and clarity, he would congratulate himself. If the dreams had been confused and powerless, such as having a falling-off-the-cliff dream, he would rescript the nightmare and replay it in his mind until he was happy with the result. Facing the cliff, he would take off and fly in skyward-soaring freedom.

Gary adopted the above exercises and reprogrammed his mind during the day so that at night he could direct himself to dream the kind of dreams he wanted to experience. Through dreaming the right dreams, he reinforced his conviction of his righteous lifestyle. Ten months after he had diligently practiced the exercise, he was approached by a business acquaintance who had invented a new concept for computer information retrieval. Three years after that, their sales were sixty million dollars.

Gary never bought that mansion with the living room that would hold his grandfather's house. He had seen himself own that mansion in one of his dreams. Now that he was financially able to make this dream come true, he no longer had the desire to prove it. Gary and his wife had really never cared about owning such an oversized house anyway; the colossal mansion was only a symbol of success that had existed in the young Gary's mind.

CONCLUSION

The dreams one has at night reflect the thoughts, jumbled or clear, that the dreamer engages in during the day. Changing the quality of your dreams at night via the Directed Dreaming exercises will change the quality of your life in your waking hours.

Before an electron can leave its first orbit, it needs to absorb sufficient energies to make its leap and reappear in a higher orbit. When it has gained its requisite momentum, it will then take the leap to claim its physical existence in the higher realm. The equivalent case of a person absorbing the necessary energy to leave an old, comfortable orbit is to simmer mentally on and experience the existence of that new orbit they want their life to take. Just as the electron absorbs its energy before making the quantum leap, humans must immerse themselves in positive dream visions, experiencing that they are living in a new environment of abundance prior to manifesting their right to claim their new life orbit.

Our Rainmaker did exactly that. In his dream state he repeatedly experienced the rains quenching the thirst of the cracked earth to bring life and rejuvenation to the villagers. You don't have to do more, you simply need to adopt the technique of Directed Dreaming: dreaming the life you want, and then living the life you dream.

SECOND SECRET

PUT YOUR MIND AT EASE

FIND WISDOM
IN IRRITATION

Before the Rainmaker acquired his power of making rain effortlessly, he was an apprentice. Like all mediocre Rainmakers, his expenditure of extraordinary effort and reaping of meager results caused him to be irritated and stressed out. Our Rainmaker, even though he was inept at creating rain early in his career, knew his irritation was the beginning of his journey to obtain greater wisdom.

When one is suffering from irritation and a stress-filled life, there is no virtue to it unless the suffering is accompanied by wisdom. Irritation is a warning to readjust our lives. It is a protection to the body, mind, and spirit. The Rainmaker needed to know how his suffering was contributing to his future ability to become a superior Rainmaker.

SEEING LIFE AS A CELESTIAL SPORT

In order to relax into life's challenges, we must step back, take a look at the big picture, and ask ourselves the serious question: If, as some cynics have said, "Life sucks and then we die," why should we even bother to live? When we have the answers to this question, we begin to take life's tests much more lightly. We may even begin to enjoy our daily struggle as a bundle of fun.

THE JOY OF COMPETITION

In the early 1900s, a peasant warlord in China was invited to visit a prestigious all-girls high school for which he was a major monetary supporter. When the warlord came to the school, he saw groups of girls fighting fiercely over a ball, running from one side of the court to the other, trying to put the ball into their respective baskets.

The warlord was furious and bellowed at the principal, "I gave you so much money to build a model school that would provide the best of everything for the students. Why don't you buy more balls so each of the girls can have one? Then they won't have to fight over just one ball!"

Why do two teams fight over a stupid ball, trying to throw it into a basket while they get their bodies bashed around and have their spirits go through the greatest of punishments? Why do humans find it is so stimulating to watch their favorite teams strain to the limits of their endurance physically and mentally?

The fun of any competitive sport is derived from the struggle to overcome opposition. Those people with the physical ability or mental talent to compete participate by playing the game; those who can't play buy tickets so they can participate vicariously in the experience of the players' struggle.

The tougher the game, the better the game. The fiercer the competition, the more people enjoy it. When the score is 95 to 10, the spectators and the players are both disappointed. When you are neck-to-neck and then win the game by only a few points, the game becomes very exhilarating.

The human spirit loves games of tough competition. Our life's encounters are identical to our competitions on the sports field. The only difference is that we think of sports competitions as games and consider business and life games as reality.

The rules of business, life, and sports are all about overcoming strong oppositional forces. The ball game becomes a metaphor for life. Problems occur when we forget that stress is an inevitable part of the human condition. Have fun while playing the game of your life.

THE NOT-SO-GREAT LIFE

My friend Pauline married the heir to one of the world's most powerful, solely-owned communications empires. Her family was featured on the television show *Lifestyles of the Rich and Famous*. Pauline often expressed the wish that she would like to be poor and have nothing. She was often in the company of her working-class artist friends so that she could experience the "fun" of their struggles. I could tell that she was truly envious of those who got to experience the full scope of being a human being hustling to make ends meet.

One of my girlfriends is married to a rich business-man. She keeps bragging to me about how fortunate and lucky she is. Her life is so smooth, so trouble-free. Yet, when I look into her eyes, I see no light, no joy, no satisfaction and happiness. If her life is truly as good as she claims it to be, why must she expend so much effort to announce it? An old Chinese apho-rism states, "Every family has a sutra (prayer) that is difficult to chant." You never have to envy other peo-ple. They all have their challenges, which might prove to be even more difficult for you to handle than the troubles you have.

LIFE HAS KEPT ITS BARGAIN

Life's challenges are never meant to devastate you. In fact, the challenges are placed before you for your en-joyment and to remind you that life has kept its side of the bargain to keep the game fun and entertaining.

Imagine if you were misinformed about the rules of football and you thought you were supposed to walk leisurely across the field with the ball while everyone else on the opposite team was supposed to keep a respectable distance from you. Suddenly, when people came from all directions, attacking you and stealing your ball, you would be horrified and furious.

Because you know the rules of football, you do not mind the attack. In fact, if the opposition force were not there, you would be disappointed that you didn't get to show off your skills at the game. Life, too, gives you the opportunity to show off—by sending adversity your way.

THE CELESTIAL GAME

Somewhere along the line, from our birth until now, we all have been misinformed. Somehow, we gained the impression that the ideal life should be without struggle. Instead, we find that life, at times, seems just plain unbearable. If life is truly terrible, why don't we just check out and tell the universe, "I no longer want to be your victim. You can play the game without me." For some mysterious reason, we are enchanted by life and cling to it with all our might. Why?

For the greater part of my life, I could not understand the real reason for human existence. You eat, you go to work or school, then you come home to sleep so that you can repeat the process all over again tomorrow. Eventually, you are old and sick, you cannot eat or sleep very well, then you die. Basically, life seemed pointless.

WHY CREATION?

Seventeen years ago, I asked a great teacher, "What is the purpose of creation? It seems so random. We try so hard to make a good living so that we can die more comfortably. If that is the case, then why don't we just die now instead of struggling until we get old and sick and more miserable?"

He answered me with the following: "For a moment, let me take your mind back to the beginning of the universe, to the place where it all started. Look, there is One Force. This One has all and lacks nothing, is infinite without limitation, pulsating with great joy, and absorbed in bliss. Some call this 'God.'

"However, for no compelling reason—for the sake

of pure sport—the One multiplies into the many. From the many, the universe comes into existence. As the great Chinese philosopher, Lao-tzu, also said: 'Tao, the Ultimate, gives birth to the One. The One gives birth to two. Two gives birth to three. Three gives birth to the ten thousand things.' A unified whole becomes the universe full of contradictions. It is a battle between the haves and have-nots, goodness and evil, intelligence and ignorance, wealth and poverty, success and failure.

"Through the process of creation, the Creative Force chooses to forget its infinite, all-knowing divine nature and takes upon itself the facet of ignorance. It plays the material game of being a limited human being. It is simultaneously eminent and transcendent.

"When this Force takes the forms of human beings, the game then becomes an attempt to regain its divine origin—the original, unified One—through the mundane living of life's challenges, the overcoming of its own self-imposed shortcomings and flaws.

"Humans are made in the image of our Creator. The characteristics of all-pervasiveness, omniscience, omnipotence, complete, unqualified love, and pure, ever-new bliss plus countless other qualities are secreted within the deep recesses of each of our hearts. Through the game of creation, the Almighty takes on the qualities of ignorance and then struggles to rediscover Oneness.

"If you are made from the substance of that Divine Power, how can you be anything but divine? Just as a lion cub raised among sheep is still a lion although he mistakenly thinks himself a sheep, so a person may think they are but a helpless human, yet their divine nature within remains unblemished and ever blissful. Even the game of struggle to realize our highest potential in the material and mental realms in our daily lives is nothing but a play manufactured by our Creator and our individual spirit.

"The power of creation caused a contraction of the universal consciousness into human consciousness; from the all-powerful, boundless power into the limited, material laws of physics. The game of creation is for the enjoyment of One and, we being one and the same with That, the spirit of humanity. Through tough competition and struggle, we learn the joy of breaking though the self-imposed human limitations and expressing our unabridged greatness."

* * *

Now that we have covered the concepts of the whole scope of creation, we get back to the original question asked above: "For what mysterious reason are we enchanted by life and cling to it with all of our might?" The short answer is that even as the mind and body are experiencing the drama of human struggle, the spirit considers this devastating struggle part of the fun.

THE STRUGGLE IS REAL

Seventeen years ago, when I heard this statement, it was merely words. Now that I am able to fully experience life as the Divine's playground, I see all is intended for everyone to grow, to expand, to have fun.

Making a bargain with omnipresence, the spirit of humanity said, "I want to have a body and be human. As spirit, I am all-pervasive and experience no suffering, no limitations. I am not bound by time, space, or the material world. I am everything. It would be so much fun to be human and pretend to be limited; to have to struggle to obtain, to overcome to obtain, to endure to obtain. Being human is so much fun."

For no other reason than the inborn desire to play, human beings participate in sports. The games may be artificial, but the struggle on the field or court is real. In the pursuit of fun, players are sometimes injured or even killed. However, the best players never lose sight of the reality that it is just a game, after all, and that they have chosen to play in it.

By the same token, you volunteer to play the game of being human in order to enjoy yourself. However, the struggle becomes unbearable when you get caught up in the game, forget who and what you really are, and fall out of touch with your divine nature. Forgetting it is just a game; you wander about this earth convinced that you are the victim of creation.

The spirit is the spark of that almighty creative power. Within, there are forces that will enable you to achieve anything to which you set your heart. For whether you manifest it or not, the spark of your divine origin remains forever alive within you.

UNDERSTANDING IS
NOT ENOUGH

To merely understand the mystery of creation is not enough—it does not help you to make rain, live your life, or run your business. The purpose of living is the game of returning to our divine nature. The closer we are to that nature, the more power we acquire to manipulate material reality, the more at ease our minds will feel about our businesses and our lives, the more savvy we become at manipulating reality.

CONCLUSION

Agitation and irritation are good states. They are signs that you have taken the essential step on the journey to discovering the Rainmaker's secret.

Even if you think you have no desire to be spiritual, you are a spiritual entity, whether you like it or not. You cannot help, at some stage in your life, seeking a reality beyond your mundane existence. In most cases this happens when your life starts to whirl out of control. Things are not going well for you on all fronts—in business or your family life. Stress and irritation are constant elements in your life. As you feel disheartened by harsh reality, you look within to the Almighty for help. Whenever things are not going well, we suddenly become very spiritual.

For most of us, at some time in our lives, we will begin this inner journey. Few are self-motivated through the pure love of humankind and the Divine. We often need a helping hand to push us into embarking on this journey. This helping hand is provided without our permission in the form of the agitation and irritation we feel in our lives. This agitation and irritation are positive signals functioning similar to pain, which warns us as a way of protecting our physical body from harm. It is a signal to tell us it is time to adjust our lives.

Our Rainmaker started from this point. It is not because he was so wise that he welcomed the pains of irritable living. Rather, after he lived through the anguish of mental agitation, material defeat, and spiritual emptiness, he came to realize that the irritation and overwhelming stress were merely the first steps toward turning to effortless achieving—the power that inevitably enhances one's ability to function more fully as a progeny of the Divine on earth.

SURRENDER
REVEALS
YOUR DESTINY

We and God have business with each other;
and in opening ourselves to His influence our
deepest destiny is fulfilled. The universe, at
those parts of it which our personal being con-
stitutes, takes a turn genuinely for the better or
for the worse in proportion as each one of us
fulfills or evades God's demands.

—William James

Confucius said, "When you are fifty years old, you should know your destiny." Fifty years old is figurative; you can be five, thirty, or sixty years old. Or you can be eighty years old and clueless about your destiny. Confucius is really communicating the concept that, if you have lived long enough, you should have made enough mistakes and accumulated enough sense to *surrender* to the will of Heaven. Only then, will you be able to see your destiny as Heaven intends it.

Before he found his occupation, our Rainmaker too made numerous wrong turns in his effort toward pursuing his righteous destiny. Every time he set his career objective on something other than being a Rainmaker, the hand of the divine would guide him back to his starting point.

But exactly how can we know our destiny? We cannot just eat rice for fifty years and earn the merit of knowing our destiny.

SURRENDER TO THE DIVINE AGENDA

Two agendas are prevalent in your life: Heaven's and yours. Often these two will clash with each other. When what we want our lives to be is different from our intended destiny, the universal will creates roadblocks. Although we may fight with all of our might in an attempt to turn the outcome to our desires, the universal will always prevails. Out of desperation, we are forced to give up or give in.

Giving in to the will of Heaven does not mean doing nothing and just accepting life as you find it. It means using your given ability, talent, and strength to do all you can to bring about a better life for yourself and others. You accept divine guidance instead of insisting on your preset notions about how things ought to be. You accept the validity of the way things are and apply your strength, possibility thinking, discrimination, and wisdom. Conversely, surrendering to defeat requires nothing more than despair, hopelessness, devastation, becoming overwhelmed by life, and finally, tossing in the towel.

True surrender comes by knowing the grand design beyond the superficial, mundane level, and thus opening up to and accepting divine guidance, allowing it to affect your life in an astoundingly positive way.

Surrendering to the Divine Will is not an easy task. Most of us go through life fighting furiously for what we think is best for us. Yet, through kindness, our Maker drags us along despite our objections.

Adults see a child's idea of the "good life" as pure

foolishness—a life with no school, no homework, and plenty of pizzas, hamburgers, candy bars, and cookies while watching television and listening to rock and roll all day. Yet we adults are no different in the eyes of the Divine. Each of us also has a definite idea of what the "good life" means that seems equally frivolous from the universal perspective. When things do not turn out to fit our mental pictures, we are devastated by our disappointment.

THERE IS NO FAILURE, ONLY DIVINE REDIRECTION

At times, we are out of tune with the grand blueprint for our intended destiny, and we desire to go into places where we don't belong. The universal force then repeatedly pushes us back to the center of the road so that we may start over again in the proper direction to better fulfill our personal destiny. Each time we have a reversal and start again, the ignorant of this world label our actions as failures.

For example, in 1984, I was at a crossroads in my career. I applied for a sales position with IBM. After a one-hour interview, they decided not to hire me. Ten years later, in 1994, I delivered a keynote address, speaking to one thousand of IBM's top sales associates at their annual acknowledgment conference in Bali.

Life is a circle within a circle in which there exist these relative incidents, erroneously identified as failures and successes, along the way. Each failure is a progression forward within the grand framework of our inevitable, complete success. Every disappointment, every failure, is guiding you in silence to your intended destiny. "Child, you are going the wrong way. This is not the path to your destiny" or "You should do it differently; your execution does not fit your talent. Polish your skills." There is no failure, only Divine redirection.

Humans will do anything to avoid so-called failure. With each experience of failing, we feel our hearts being broken into many fragments. One thing is certain: When the Creator is pleased with you, he will take a special interest in you. He will make sure your heart gets cracked open because only when the heart is broken and the resistive ego cracked can we let in the light of wisdom. For those extraordinary people exalted to the highest splendor, the Creator will raise the hammer, crack their hearts, and take residence within.

DESTINY REVEALS ITSELF IN THREE PHASES

Since human beings are resistant creatures, we do not give up our agenda until we engage Fate in an arm-wrestling match. When we surrender to Fate's arm, we win. On the other hand, when we win the arm-wrestling contest with Fate, we lose—those who have put up a gallant fight and won their battle with Fate forever remain in darkness about their destiny. These people generally work hard and earn their money but without satisfaction. For most people, destiny reveals itself through the following three phases.

PHASE ONE
YOU ARE HUNGRY

It all starts when you feel dissatisfied with life. Without a sufficiently large appetite for life, there is no motivation toward action. If you do not act, nothing happens—you vegetate and die. Even the simple act of eating requires the will to action. In the initial phase of your pursuit of personal success, you will find that you are enthusiastically motivated. Your actions are driven by a self-centered desire, and they vibrate with a single voice of "I want, I want, I want."

By being hungry, you will obtain certain objects of your desires. The power of hunger will motivate you to exercise your will, and you will be off to a good start. At this stage, you are winning the wrestling match. Your score is 1; Fate, 0.

However, when you have lived long enough and enjoyed a certain amount of success in fulfilling your desires, you often discover that you are not totally happy in this phase. In fact, you may find that you are more confused and miserable now than ever. This all happens to you because Fate is good and kind, and you have been extremely lucky. It is a sign that the Universe is taking a personal interest in you and readjusting your course so that you may achieve way beyond your present meager successes. You are being pushed into the second phase.

PHASE TWO
THE TURNING POINT

Phase two is often caused by some kind of dramatic turning point in one's life such as a personal tragedy, the loss of a loved one, professional setbacks, or financial failure. As a matter of fact, whatever you care the most about, whatever hurts you the most, will happen. Motivated by your experience of pain, you will begin your inner quest. It is true—when things are going badly, we became more spiritual.

When you begin this inner search, you become overwhelmed by your own character defects and pettiness. It is like being in a room where there is no sunlight and, therefore, you see no dirt. And then, when the drapes are pulled back a little, the sunlight pours in. Suddenly you discover that everything in the room is covered with dust; even the air is filled with dust particles. In fact, it is not that the room was clean before—the room has always been the same old dirty room—you only see the dirt now because the light has begun to illuminate the room. Not until you are able to see the dirt can you have any hope of cleaning it up.

In the classic movie *The Reutrn of the Jedi,* the young Luke Skywalker feared facing Darth Vader, his powerful and evil enemy. His teacher Obi-Wan Kenobi told him, "To be a Jedi, Luke, you must confront and then go beyond the dark side." In the beginning of the film, Luke Skywalker was a boy. At the end of the film, after he had confronted the dark side, he started to gain texture. Confronting the dark side (within and without) is the beginning of phase two. This is the phase that ignites the rocket of transformation.

However, this is also the most dangerous and threatening phase. So many people get stuck at phase two, defeated by it, and end up as failures because they fight hardship instead of letting it guide them. Movement from phase one to phase two does not require your intervention—Fate shoves your face into your own dirt. It is up to you to pull yourself up from phase two into three.

Phase two is not sent to defeat you. Rather, it is the cleansing process you must pass through so that you can proceed on to phase three and experience a much higher, refined degree of personal excellence. There are success stories that we encounter every day that can be ascribed to temporary good luck. However, no person who has enjoyed true and lasting success, who has left a legacy of progress and goodness for the world, has ever been spared from walking through the dark valley of phase two; fate wins, you lose. When the score is Fate, 1; you, 1, you are on your way to fulfilling your destiny.

PHASE THREE
DESTINY REVEALED

You realize that what is supposed to be yours no one can take away, delay, or stop from coming to you. You know that your success does not depend on certain individuals or circumstances but on the ever generous pouring forth from the cornucopia of the universal abundance. You know that destiny is your servant as well as your master.

You perform your duty in harmony with the Divine will, and therefore you can disregard the state of the moment-to-moment results. You know that everything you have done will eventually and inevitably lead toward the ultimate completeness of your material and spiritual rewards. At this point, your score total is 1; Fate, 2. You surrender, therefore, you win.

This is a highly evolved state that may seem paradoxical or impossible when one is stuck in a prior phase. Be assured, however, that this is the state of mind that the women and men of destiny share and the state that lies dormant in each human soul, waiting to be activated.

GEORGE WASHINGTON'S JOURNEY

George Washington's life followed exactly the three phases described above. In most people's lives, the three phases are not so well defined and clearly distinguishable; there are inevitable overlaps. In Washington's life, these phases happened in a clear-cut, precise order.

Whether you attended grade school in the United States or elsewhere, the story of young George Washington chopping down the cherry tree was ubiquitous. This story gave Washington such an aura of holiness that we mere mortals felt inadequate when our virtues did not compare to the pure seed of greatness that had been planted in the breast of this extraordinary child. In fact, according to historians, this story is a fiction manufactured by a clergyman toward inspiring the children who attended his church's Sunday school classes to follow the path of honesty. The real story of the real man named George Washington is a tale of quite a different type.

The life story of George Washington reveals a man who evolved from a swindler to an icon who finally embodied true, altruistic greatness. As we get in touch with the human side of Washington's life story, our admiration is not tarnished. Instead, it expands into the realization of how truly great was the stature of this Father of America. As Abraham Lincoln said of Washington, "To add brightness to the sun or glory to the name of Washington is impossible."

PHASE ONE:
GEORGE WAS HUNGRY

DESTINY'S SETBACKS

When Washington was eleven, his father died. His two elder half-brothers, Lawrence and Augustine, received most of their father's estate. Also, they both were sent to England for the best of educations. The teenager, George, without the edge of wealth and a proper formal education, set out to make his mark on the world stage.

When George was sixteen, Lawrence invited him to live at Mount Vernon. Lawrence, then thirty, was a major in the Virginia militia and served as a member of the House of Burgesses, the governing body of that colony. He had married into one of the wealthiest families in the territory. Young George found his brother Lawrence's lavish lifestyle much to his liking. Washington was proud of his brother and felt that he, too, deserved everything that his brother had— the status of gentleman, copious wealth, and a well-landed estate. In an eighteenth-century Virginian's life, nothing was more valued than the attainment of this coveted status.

Young George conducted himself with great maturity. While he lived at Mount Vernon and enjoyed the life of a Virginia squire, his young mind was busy mapping his path to wealth and designing his future so that he could continue living in the manner to which he was fast becoming accustomed.

COLLECTING THE SYMBOLS
OF SUCCESS

George was obsessed in these younger years with the idea of being a proper "gentleman." Even in his early years, he had started to collect the "symbols" of the gentleman.

To Be a Gentleman, One Must Have a Gentlemanly Occupation

In Washington's time, being a land surveyor was an important and prestigious position, equal in stature to that of physician or clergyman. In 1749, at the age of seventeen, George passed his examination and officially filed his commission as a land surveyor.

A Gentleman Must Have Land— the More, the Better

Working as a surveyor, George was well paid. By the time he was twenty, he owned 2,008 acres of the most fertile land in the area. Being a surveyor, he naturally got to pick for himself the best parcels of land.

Washington's acreage was not all obtained through honest work. At the beginning of the French and Indian War, the governor of Virginia, in order to entice the colonists to fight, promised land to all of the enlisted men. The offer did not include the officers, on whom, as gentlemen, the governor was counting to serve out of their sense of aristocratic honor.

By the end of the eight-year French and Indian War, a new governor had arrived who was not familiar with the details of the previous governor's promise. George and his fellow officers conspired together and were able to change the old proclamation that had granted land to the enlisted men into granting it to the officers.

Through this cheap swindle, at a great cost to those men whom he had commanded, Washington obtained an additional twenty thousand acres of prime fertile land.

A Gentleman Must Have
a Gentleman's Wife

At the age of twenty-seven, George married a woman truly worthy of being a gentleman's wife: Martha Curtis, a twenty-eight-year-old lady who happened to be the wealthiest widow in Virginia. Possessing money and position, she had all the apparatuses of prestige that George had always chased. Through this marriage, George gained the status of a true gentleman.

A Gentleman Must Have Gentlemanly Company

Armed with a gentleman's wife, Washington began entertaining his neighbors at Mount Vernon. He gave lavish parties, inviting those who could help him promote himself and expedite his ambitions. He was constantly pursuing the opportunity to rub elbows with the rich, the famous, and the powerful.

A Gentleman Must Have Political and Social Position

Following in his brother Lawrence's footsteps, George ran for the House of Burgesses. He lost the first time because, on the day of the election, he did not serve liquor to the voters, as was customarily done. The second time he ran, he made sure that the bar was generously stocked and open to all voters. It worked liked a charm; he was elected to the governing body of the colony of Virginia.

A GENTLEMAN MUST WEAR
THE RED COAT

Washington served in the Virginia militia at the rank of major and was eventually promoted to commander. But the rank of commander in the Virginia militia was nothing compared to becoming a British officer —the true mark of a gentleman. Throughout his life, George had craved a position in the British army.

Washington's only military education had consisted of reading two art-of-war books and, in his spare time, taking fencing lessons. But this lack of formal military training never stopped him from desiring to wear the distinguished red coat of the British officer.

After repeated requests and subsequent rejections, Washington gave up the idea of being a British officer, convinced that he was being discriminated against because he was a colonist. This obsessive desire to be a British officer played a major role in the shaping of his destiny.

WASHINGTON'S CHARACTER DEFECTS

In the first phase of his life, Washington was totally ignorant of his numerous personality defects.

His Vanity

When Washington received his first military assignment in 1754 during the French and Indian War, he thought this was his big chance to be recognized by the powers that be. Washington established Fort Necessity in the Great Meadows at the Forks of Ohio. At the first rainstorms, flooding had George and his men up to their knees in mud and water, which compelled them to give up the fort and surrender to the French.

Washington signed the surrender document, which was written in French. Not being conversant in that language, he did not realize that he had signed an admission of guilt that, in a previous battle, he had assassinated a French diplomat after that gentleman had surrendered to him and was being held as his prisoner.

The document referred to an incident precipitated by an Indian chief who, while fighting on the side of the English and assisting Washington, charged without warning into the circle of French prisoners and bashed in the head of the diplomat with his tomahawk.

In order to reply to the charges and offer the correct explanation, Washington would have had to admit that he was not knowledgeable in French. Since it was the mark of a true English gentleman in those days to be able to speak and write French fluently, he was not about to admit that.

His Habit of Blaming Others

Clearly, Washington's first chance to be recognized as a great commander had turned out badly. In his defense, he promptly blamed the officer whom he had picked to be his translator for his poor translation job. Of course, since Washington could not read French, he had no business picking his own French translator. He then blamed his superior, who had sent him to do battle at the Forks.

Throughout his life, when circumstances did not transpire according to his vision, Washington would find others to blame. When he met with failure and difficulties, he would always feel victimized and double-crossed.

His Craving for Recognition

At the age of twenty, Washington rode to Williamsburg for an audience with Governor Dinwiddie. There, he requested that he be appointed to the Virginia militia at the rank of major. For a man with no military training, what he was asking was a tall order, and his request was turned down. Eventually, the rank of major was granted to George when he was given the peaceful and least strategic portion of southern Virginia to defend.

Even then, his title was not given based upon his merit. It came about because of his relationship with the notable Lord Thomas Fairfax, a distant relative by marriage. Furthermore, Governor Dinwiddie was a business partner with George's brother, Lawrence. Because of this, no one took Washington seriously in the regiment. Even the junior officers did not want to obey him.

In 1775, Washington represented Virginia at the Continental Congress in Philadelphia. The focus of the discussion was taxation without representation and the British occupation.

Washington did not come to the meeting without his own agenda. He was the only delegate in the hall who dressed in the heroic military uniform of a general—one that he designed and had tailored for himself, distinguished epaulets and all.

It is said that before others can perceive you as fit for the role in life you wish to play, you must first dress the part, act the part, and become the part. Now Washington saw the opportunity to fulfill his deepest desire. He thought that if the members of the Congress saw him in this uniform, they would see him as the man best qualified to be the commander of the Army of the Continental Congress.

Just as Washington had anticipated, the delegates realized he was exactly what they needed. He was young enough (forty-three); he was experienced in battle (mostly in defeat); he was on the right side of political compromise—a soldier from Virginia at a time when the Congress needed to persuade the Southern colonies to join in this freedom fight; and he had his own uniform.

Historians call Washington a great actor. I call him an exceptional salesman. He sold believability and vision. The score was Washington 1, Fate 0.

PHASE TWO
DESPAIR

A TIME FOR FEAR

George was soon on the road to Boston, carrying the commission papers that gave him command over the hastily forming Continental army. All of his life, Washington had craved the recognition bestowed upon him by Congress. Now the reality hit home. As he looked at himself in brutal honesty, he saw only a tobacco farmer; he knew how to grow quality tobacco. But to face well-trained, professional fighting men, he had to admit to himself that he knew little of the art of war.

Arriving in Boston, his worst fears took flesh. Where he had hoped to find the great soldiers of a revolution ready to liberate America, he found only an unkempt, ragtag bunch of greenhorn farmers, trained to raise crops and cattle, not to kill men on the battlefield. He greatly despaired. How could he lead this herd of sheep to be slaughtered by the trained, professional soldiers of Britain, the greatest conquering army in the world?

MIRROR OF HIS INADEQUACY

The British sailed to New York to engage Washington's army. The battles fought in New York showed Washington that his fears were well justified. His military training (from the two books he had read) proved quite inadequate. His poorly trained army was easy pickings for the crack British troops. Getting their first taste of real battle—the blood, the gore, the screams of the dying—many of his soldiers deserted.

Washington entered a state of depression. He saw himself not as a great general but as a fake. This defeat on the battlefield was a reflection of the defeat he felt within himself at his attempt to become someone of great importance. Now there were no likely suspects available for him to blame. Previously, he had always found a convenient scapegoat; here, in his greatest defeat, he stood utterly alone.

BATTLING WITH THE GENERALS

To add to his myriad problems, he was forced to fight battles on two fronts: one against the British and the other against his own generals. Since most of his generals had been trained and had served tours of duty in the British army, they thought this bucolic upstart an interloper and a fool—inadequate to command a herd of cows, much less a distinguished group of military tacticians such as themselves. They conspired to remove him by surreptitiously sending Congress venomous reports requesting that he be replaced, while at the same time they openly defied his orders and fought him at every turn.

By the end of 1776, the situation had become so hopeless and desperate that Washington had to consider the possibility of running out west to hide. In a letter to his cousin, he wrote, "I see the impossibility of serving with reputation. I was never in such unhappiness since I was born." In a letter to his younger brother, Jack, he was even more honest and frank: "I think the game is pretty near over." The score was now Washington 1, Fate 1.

PHASE THREE
SURRENDERING TO HIS DESTINY

DEFEATING THE DEMONS WITHIN

More horrible to Washington than defeat or death was the thought that he would have to accept the reality of being a nobody, a nothing, a fake. He had struggled all of his life trying to prove to himself and others that he was a man of importance and worthy of respect. Now the mirror of self-reflection was facing him; the pain of defeat was forcing him to take a long, hard look at himself.

He realized that if one expects to be respected, one must respect himself first. He must be a man of true substance—something more than the stuff and symbols he had gathered around himself for the purpose of being respectable. Before Washington could defeat the British, he had to defeat the demons of his own mind. Before he could achieve victory over the world, he had to triumph over himself.

TURNING INWARD

In December 1776, Washington was in serious trouble. His soldiers' enlistment time was up, and they were about to go home. So far, he had seen nothing but defeat. In desperation, George Washington, the man, turned inward to consult with George Washington, the spirit.

Dreading the loss of a reputation that had taken him a lifetime to build, Washington sank into the agony in the pit of his soul. In this condition of resignation, his mind stopped racing and became still. He became detached and, in this state, discerned the true meaning of honor and recognition.

They had nothing to do with all the symbols he had collected, such as the large house, land, and social and political status. They had only to do with whether a man is willing to do Fate's bidding—to fulfill the duty and role his Maker has assigned to him in this life.

GEORGE DISCOVERS THE AXIOM OF INNER COMPLETENESS

By getting in touch with his own spirit, Washington was in turn touched by Fate. He saw that his blind, vigorous pursuit of becoming a respectable gentleman was rooted in his lack of the sense of completeness within himself.

George knew he could not win the war by fighting for all the wrong reasons. The things that had been so important—reputation, status, a royal commission—were as insignificant as not being able to read French. From here, he could see to the far horizon of the future, and he saw that the role that had been entrusted to him was so grand, even death would be a meager price to pay.

Once he had given up the burden of vanity, his mind was sharply focused. Every cell of his body and brain were aligned with his soul's cry of victory for this noblest of causes. Now he would fight effectively because it was his divine duty to fight. It was his destiny to win this war for the noble, fledgling republic struggling to be born on the shores of the continent called America.

With the turning around of Washington's inner state, so too turned the fate of the American Revolution. On that freezing Christmas Eve in 1776, Washington single-handedly altered the course of American history.

THE TURNING POINT

With twenty-four hundred men, he crossed the Delaware River in the midst of a snowstorm to mount a sneak attack. His battle cry was "Death or Victory." He and his men were grimly determined to turn the war around or die in the attempt.

That Christmas Eve was the beginning of the transmuting of defeat into victory. Washington abandoned aristocratic honor by turning from the rules of traditional warfare to the use of deceptive tactics in order to obtain victory. He arrived with his men at the enemy camp at 3:00 in the morning. The enemy, Hessian mercenaries sleeping off a night of unbridled drunken revelry, were unprepared. It was a complete rout.

THE BIRTH OF A TRUE LEADER

In April 1781, the British were attacking in Virginia and had their cannons trained on Washington's estate at Mount Vernon. Thomas Jefferson, then the governor of Virginia, told Washington to come home and mount a defense for his home and state. Sitting at his camp on the Hudson River, Washington declined. He had grown dispassionate about small victories. He knew that the pivotal point of his military operation was where he was, up north. His intention was to win the war, not the battle.

Washington had become totally unconcerned about his possessions at Mount Vernon. He removed his identification from his beloved estate in Virginia; he was no longer a Virginian. Washington was now a man of destiny, a citizen of the American republic, the future country for whose birth he was selflessly fighting.

The fight between Washington's revolutionary army and the British Empire was a war that tested to the limits both participants' endurance. To win, Washington knew that he had to outlast England's appetite for war. Washington was aware that he could not really defeat this superior enemy in the battlefield; he knew that he must outlast them by enduring longer and greater hardships than they were willing to.

Washington and his American revolutionary army sustained their spirit through to the last significant battle of the American Revolution—the three-week siege of Yorktown—and there, bowing to the superior desire, will, and purpose of the colonists, the British army surrendered.

EMBRACING DESTINY

On March 15, 1783, he was in his quarters, furiously preparing a speech powerful enough to stop a civil war. His generals were not willing to hand over the victory and power to a Continental Congress that had done nothing but lie to them throughout the course of the war.

Now the generals wanted to storm Congress, guns loaded, to demand their back pay. They intended to create a form of dictatorial government and declare Washington the king. George Washington, the man who had been driven totally by his search for the status of gentleman and the commission of an English officer, now had the opportunity to be king, an equal to George III. But the Washington of yesterday was no longer alive in this new Washington.

Standing before his men, Washington read his carefully prepared speech and the letter he had just received from the Congress, which promised once again to pay their back wages. As he concluded, he looked into their eyes and saw that they had not been convinced. The powers of persuasion, spirit, and eloquence that had induced his men to follow him through freezing winters, starvation, and bloody battles failed him in the glow of victory.

The air was heavy and suffocating. The crowd of soldiers pressed closer, all eyes upon him. Washington stopped. He then did an extraordinary thing. Slowly, he removed a pair of glasses from his coat pocket. His men had never seen him wearing glasses; they were shocked at this sign of frailty in their invincible leader.

Washington looked up and said, "Gentlemen, you will forgive the spectacles. Not only have I grown gray in your service; now I find myself going blind." With these few words, he touched their hearts and brought tears to the eyes of these rock-hard, seasoned fighting men. The glasses symbolized how he had given up everything—his youth, his life, his fortune—for the cause of victory; by betraying their noble cause through rash action, they would also betray him who had given all he had.

At this moment, as he referred to his eyesight and his personal sacrifice for the revolution, he was reminding his men of the price they had already paid for the ideal of the republic. The republic was greater than the Congress that hadn't paid them. His gesture also reminded his men how together they had contributed to the founding of their new nation and that it wasn't the time to forsake their destiny. By abandoning the kingship, he embraced his divine destiny in history.

Historians regard this scene as an extraordinary political performance. I see it as going beyond performance. This was the moment that George Washington, the man, merged with his destiny to become the

Father of the Nation. Most people thought that Washington had a flawless character. As we have seen, he had just as many human flaws and carried as much emotional baggage as anyone else. Yet, in spite of himself and his character defects, by learning from life's trials and tribulations, he ultimately evolved into a heroic man of destiny. He surrendered to Heaven's will over his own, making the score Washington 1, Fate 2—a true victory.

THE BEGINNING OF SURRENDER

Surrender is the essential element necessary for knowing your destiny and moving from the second phase to the third phase. The caveat is: True surrender always comes with a big price tag. The universe never means to hurt you, but when it redirects you to the high road, you often feel the sting of its touch. In the Hindu scriptures, the story is told of Lord Shiva stirring up the ocean of human consciousness. When the poison sediment of evil tendencies that had been accumulating over the years at the bottom of that

mental sea surfaced, the previously crystal-clear water became deeply clouded. In a move to save humankind from folly, Lord Shiva drank the murky,
lethal, deposit-filled liquid, and His throat turned
blue when the poison lodged there.

In this story Shiva represents our human spirit stirring up the submerged dirt in our mental sea. If we
do not deal with our subconscious shortcomings, we
end up living in an ignorantly blissful state. All we
see within ourselves is factitious goodness. In this
state of personal self-righteousness, we—and those
who agree with us and believe like us—are "right,"
and the rest of the world is "wrong."

When phase two, the turning point, comes, we are
forced to look at ourselves with an objective, critical
eye and see what is really there. We then disturb the
quicksand sediments of our mind, and as happened
when Lord Shiva stirred the ocean of human consciousness, our dirt begins to surface. This is the beginning of the inner transformation, the beginning of
the battle for surrender.

THREE STEPS TO DIVINE SURRENDER

To say it briefly and clearly, so that there may be no doubt: God in His faithfulness gives each man what is best for him.

—Meister Eckhart

Everyone's life contains a certain amount of unexpected tragedy, and we find that when one surrenders to Heaven's will, magically, all turns out for the best. Even the loss of a loved one or financial disaster can bring triumph. The intensity of life's dramas may vary, but the three steps that take us from phase two to phase three, the noble state of divine surrender, are the same.

STEP 1
DESPERATION

Everything seems out of control. Nothing goes the way it is "supposed" to. You are doing everything you can, trying to control and fix it. Even with all of your intelligence, determination, and strength, you cannot reverse the set course.

STEP 2
DETACHMENT

Out of desperation you want to give up. At this stage some simply quit and cave in, never to move out of the state of defeat. Those who give up out of hopelessness stop struggling and yet still hold on to their old picture of how life ought to be and complain that it is not that way. They are stuck there until the grave, while others gain the wisdom of detachment. People who are detached are not crushed by life's setbacks: They don't give up. They discover the hidden treasure in the hopeless situation and then redirect their energies to follow the current, swimming with the force of the waves.

When you are detached, you enter into the state of witness. While you are adjusting your course, forsaking your old ways, relearning the rhythm of the forces occurring around you and engaging in positive actions, another part of you is witnessing the rise and fall of the human drama without enmity or affection.

When I first experienced this state of "I don't care so much," I was quite alarmed. I asked, "How can I get ahead if part of me seems to not really care? If I really don't care that much about gain and loss, how can I motivate myself to work with enthusiasm?"

123

Then I noticed that when I "don't care" a great deal about the outcome or the process, my performance is raised to a new level of excellence with clarity and ease. True excellence is not born out of struggle and desperation; rather it comes from the place of calm that is born out of divine surrender.

STEP 3
DIVINE SURRENDER

When you surrender to the power of the Almighty and embrace the true essence of "Let Thy will be done," you perform your duty without agitation or desire, yet your actions will benefit yourself and others. You will become the earthly vehicle for the will of heaven.

THE PATH TO OVERCOMING EMOTIONAL TURBULENCE

While you are battling for surrender, the following five points can help to alleviate the pain of riding your emotional roller coaster:

1

AVOID SUPPRESSION

Drop the twin burdens of failure and success. This does not mean that you won't experience your emotions of joy upon achieving or of agony upon defeat, but you will observe them objectively.

A friend of mine recently brought up the subtext of how the Japanese tend to suppress their emotions. The root of this behavior is to be found within the Buddhist tradition. In spiritual pursuits, the seeker should be able to totally detach his emotion from the joy of gain and the agony of loss. To the samurai warrior, the highest ancient social class and the role model for Japan's present-day populace, expressing the emotions of joy or sadness was considered inferior. A samurai was expected to view joy and sadness as equal and remain aloof from both.

However, as many noble ideas suffer upon contact with the masses, misconceptions have occurred and well-intentioned traditions have been distorted. Instead of striving to achieve an inner detachment from their emotions, many Japanese practice an outer suppression of their emotions, to the detriment of their health.

2

WALK THROUGH THE DARK VALLEY

The sublime indifference to one's high and low emotions is often reached by a willingness to walk through the dark valley of human emotion, to examine unabashed the core of our pain and agony. While we are acting out our agonies and ecstasies, a part of us is just watching the show. We are the audience as well as the actor. With practice, playing the two roles simultaneously will come naturally.

By watching and witnessing our reactions to events, we gain an understanding of ourselves. In time, we place less and less importance on our highs and lows, joys and sorrows, gains and losses.

3

LET YOUR FINGERS DO THE TALKING

Try writing down how you feel. If you have had the experience of writing down your emotions, you know that often what you intend to write may be very different from what you actually end up writing. You will discover that your fingers have a mind of their own. You might think you know how you feel until you see your mind directing your fingers to write things that you never thought were in your head.

If you have never written about your feelings before, give it a try. Do not try to write; just write. You don't even have to write a complete sentence. Transmit your feelings from your heart to your fingers and then out to the paper. If you spend ten thousand dollars on the couch of a psychoanalyst, he or she will prescribe for you to keep a journal of your feelings. After all, the psychiatrist knows he or she cannot heal you—it is up to you to discover your own feelings and then heal yourself.

4
ACCEPT THAT NOTHING
HAPPENS BY ACCIDENT

Only one thing is certain: Life is ever changing. Through change, nature evolves and human wisdom progresses. Nothing in this world is an accident. Every seemingly insignificant event hides a profound mystery that is waiting to be discovered. Not a single leaf dares fall without Heaven's permission. Through unexpected incidents, the universe tries to teach you something. Learn the lessons.

5

CELEBRATE YOUR BROKEN HEART

Rejoice and celebrate each time your heart is broken. Only when your heart is broken can the light enter. Not until you have felt the pain of suffering can you know how others suffer. This is where you learn empathy. This is when others can look into your eyes, the windows of the soul, and see texture, wisdom, compassion, and refinement. After the experience of a broken heart you became more beautiful and more attractive to the world.

CONCLUSION

Life is a school. Unless you complete your lessons at each phase, you don't get to move forward. One's life becomes repetitive by dealing with the same old tired lessons. Some will never arrive at the third phase during this lifetime; they will only toy around between the first and second phases.

However, for those who are willing to grow, the Divine hands are willing and eager to interfere and throw you forward, in spite of yourself. Attack the circumstances in which Fate has placed you with diligence and courage. Life is designed for you to win, even though the odds against you seem insurmountable. Like Washington, our meager desires can also ignite explosive transformations into the highest of ideals and destinies. Every apparent dead end and misstep will ultimately turn out to have been necessary.

When questioned, "How did you discover your destiny?", the Rainmaker replied that he had simply asked the universal Being to make clear his way. Through your willingness to surrender, you are letting in the Light of the Divine. Allow its hand to guide you and destiny will reveal itself.

LIVE TO THRIVE, NOT JUST SURVIVE

Just imagine if our Rainmaker had thought to himself when he entered the village, "I better do a good job making rain. If I don't cause the rain to fall, the villagers will be very upset with me. They will demand their money back. They will tell other villages that I am a lousy Rainmaker, that I am a fake. Then, my reputation will be ruined. My business will fail; my creditors will come after me. I may be forced to declare bankruptcy. I will lose face and bring shame to my family. My wife will divorce me. She will take my kids, my house, my savings. I'm doomed. Oh, God, please let it rain for me; if you don't, I'll have to kill myself. No, I don't really have the guts to kill myself. But, I don't have the guts to live either. . . . Why

don't you send a little rain? . . . You are so stingy. . . .
A little rain won't hurt you . . . damn it, rain! I am
sorry, I shouldn't curse the Almighty. I take it back.
Forgive my sins. But . . . why can't you just send a little rain? If you let it rain this time, I will donate 10
percent of my total income every year to your church.
Okay, okay, 25 percent . . . is that gross or net? Please,
I beg of you . . ." Of course this would not be the way
to bring harmony to himself or to the villagers.

Fear of not being able to survive paralyzes us from
engaging with life; it holds us back from everything
we attempt to accomplish. A corporation's survival de-
pends on individual performance, and yet employees
often suffocate under the fear that they cannot survive.
Instead we learn small, timid behaviors that are calculated to preserve our survival—and destined to protect
us from leading more creative, fulfilling lives.

BE WILLING
NOT TO SURVIVE

Terri is a young professional who opened a com-
puter-graphics consulting business with his partner,

Gregory. Both partners needed to do the office's odd jobs such as addressing shipping labels, taping boxes for shipping, organizing files and disks, dropping the mail at the post office. Terri's error rate at performing these simple jobs—tasks that most ten-year-olds could accomplish at 95 percent accuracy—was around 60 percent. His excuse was, "I am not good at mundane tasks." Yet these mundane tasks were not brain surgery or rocket science that certain people just couldn't master due to lack of ability.

His error rate was so grossly high that Gregory always had to salvage his mistakes. Once Terri taped the top of a shipping box without taping the bottom. When the box arrived at the customer's site, there was nothing in it. He was a walking disaster. Whenever he touched something, chaos ensued and damage control followed. Terri's lack of respect for doing the "mundane" work caused many arguments between the two partners. They could not afford to hire an outside helper to do the jobs that Terri was supposed to be able to handle. Out of desperation, Gregory insisted Terri participate in a self-help workshop. During the workshop, the truth flashed to Terri.

In Terri's mind, he felt he was a "slave" when doing mundane work. In order to resist being a slave, he learned from a very young age to screw up every mundane task ever assigned to him. In this way, no one would ever hire him as a potential "labor" worker. The only problem was that he became so convinced that he had to screw up the simple tasks to enhance his opportunity for personal survival that he ended up sabotaging his and his partner's business.

Liz is a business-equipment salesperson who used an opposite, equally self-sabotaging tactic. She figured the way to make herself very important to her sales manager, so that her manager couldn't do without her, was to withhold information from her boss. Whenever her boss tried to get information on a particular customer from her, it was like pulling teeth. She always told as little as possible. Eventually her boss got tired of her manipulation and told her, "As long you think you need to survive by manipulating and withholding information from me, you'll be out the door very quickly. You must serve me the way I want to be served, not the way your mind has calculated how to enhance its chance for personal survival."

BE WILLING TO FACE THE WORST CONSEQUENCES

As long as you are clinging to life at all costs, there is no peace or harmony. The more you fear not surviving, the tighter you cling to ill-calculated survival strategies until you squeeze the very life out of everything you do. Eventually, simple tasks are blown out of proportion in your mind into life-or-death situations, and you shut out joy and vitality from your life.

The thirteenth-century Hindu philosopher Shankaracharya said, "Even the greatest warrior, when standing in the midst of the battlefield, sweats with fear. However, while his body is fearful and his mind is fearful, his spirit is fearless." I have never been in the midst of a battle with bombs exploding over my head and bullets dancing all around me, but when I watch a war film I often ask myself the serious question, "What would I do if I were in that battle?" I would probably be busy looking for the deepest hole in which to hide. Yes, that would be my first instinct. Nonetheless, when I realized there was no use hiding, I would probably grasp onto the spirit of death and do my duty.

135

As soon as I switch my mind from the fear of being harmed to embracing the spirit of death, immediately the fear flees and death becomes my protector. In this state, I feel so much more alive and powerful.

In the trials of your life, instead of acting gutless, embrace the possibility of not surviving and be willing to face the worst of consequences. You will find there a sudden burst of blissful courage that is rooted in your willingness to not survive. When you see death as the sublime manifestation of the Creator, the identical twin to birth, then death is not so horrible. When you are truly willing to face death, its spirit will protect you from the fear of being harmed. Often it seems that on the battlefield all the bullets are aimed at the biggest cowards.

DEATH WILL PROTECT
YOU FROM HARM

My assistant, Tim, told me of an incident that occurred one night after a speaking engagement in Washington, D.C. Walking back to his hotel, he took a route that traversed a neighborhood located on the fringe of an area known for its riots. As he ambled along, he noticed he was being followed by about a dozen gang members.

The faster he walked, the faster they pursued him. A chase ensued. Tim found himself running deeper into an area of D.C. that was foreign to him. Right on his heels, they were chasing him relentlessly. He thought to himself, "Well, this is it." He began to accept the possibility that tonight would be the night he would die.

In a flash of inspiration, he abruptly stopped running and turned to face the gang. An idea blazed luminously in his mind—if he must die at this moment, his death was not his end. And since his death was not the end, it must at least be the beginning of some new experience. In short, quite possibly, death would not be so bad after all. As the Sufi poet Rumi said, "My death is my wedding with eternity."

The gang felt the fearlessness within Tim. With the intimidation element removed from the space, the thrill of experiencing their power to harm had vanished.

The leader of the gang dropped his menacing stance, stepped forward, and stretching out his hand, said, "What's up, man?" They shook hands and then walked their separate ways. Tim's new friend, death, had defended him.

The principle that Tim applied on the street also works in life in general. The more fearful you are about your survival, the more mistakes you will tend to make. When you are willing to focus on the duty, risk, exhilaration, and fun of doing it rather than on the fear of making mistakes, you will begin to understand the meaning of thriving.

LIVING WELL, DYING WELL

A great saint said, "The purpose of living is to prepare for the moment of death. By preparing for death, one learns how to live well."

Similarly, when one of Confucius's students asked him how to honor the spirits, Confucius replied, "You do not even know how to honor mankind, how can you think of honoring the spirits?" Then the student asked, "May I ask what will happen when I die?" Confucius replied, "When you do not know how to live, how can you ask about how to die?"

Only in living well can one learn how to die. However, in order to live well, one must conquer the fear of living, which is rooted in the fear of death. This fear is manifested in millions of faces as fearing to make decisions, fearing to take calculated risks, fearing commitment, fearing mistakes, fearing confrontation, fearing life, fearing fear. Living boldly and well is not derived from linear logic; it is a truism experienced by befriending death.

DEATH WILL COME
TO YOUR RESCUE

Imagine that a divine messenger comes to you and tells you that you are going to die one year from now. She says, "For the next year, you will enjoy good health, and your death will be painless. Your only job now is to live a harmonious life. However, you must work. You cannot go out, charge up your credit cards, and blow your savings accounts."

Make a list of what your life would be like for the next year. Then make another list of what your life would be like if you carried on your business as usual. Compare the two lists. Ask yourself the question, what makes the two lists so different? The answer probably has something to do with fear. Due to your fear of suffering the consequences of doing the wrong thing, making the wrong decisions, you jeopardize your personal and career survival. So you handle your work and life with "business as usual."

If you knew you were going to die soon, you would not be so concerned about survival. Even if you made mistakes, the consequences would not be so awful, because death would come to your rescue. But whether it be one year, three years, or thirty years, death will always come to your rescue. What is there to fear? The worst that can happen is death, and when you truly know what death is, that is not such a bad option.

For the people who have encountered death and have returned to tell their stories, the one thing they all have in common is that they no longer operate their lives timidly. They open themselves up for challenges. They receive life as an adventure instead of a torturous ordeal. Suddenly, their business and personal lives are full of choice and freedom. You often hear stories about people who, having encountered a death experience, state that their life, their business, their relationships, everything got better.

As Jack London said, "The proper function of man is to live, not to exist." The only reason we find ourselves existing instead of living life is that we are blocked by fear of not surviving. When we befriend death, it protects us from the inherent harm in the world. This creates tremendous freedom and peace in our hearts.

CONTEMPLATING DEATH CREATES HARMONY

When I was young, living in Taiwan, I was a die-hard Catholic. I spent every day for over ten years contemplating the death of Christ. I found that by contemplating death, one learns a great deal about living. The following is a partial list of benefits that lead to the inner harmony I have seen manifest unfailingly when one spends time considering the state of death. I am sure you will be able to add more to this list:

- It keeps us focused on what is truly important in our daily lives.
- It puts problems in their proper perspective so they seem less troublesome.
- It decreases our stress level.
- It intensifies our connectedness with our Creator.
- It cultivates the profound state of detachment from loss and gain. It gives us equal vision about temporary success and failure.
- It fortifies within us the freedom and courage to do what we are supposed to do—not what is expedient and comfortable.
- It crystallizes within us the conviction that the purpose of life is to prepare us for the moment of death; therefore, how we live each moment matters.
- It gives us fearlessness, for the source of all fear is rooted in the fear of death.
- Most of all, it will break our survival mode so that we can enjoy and thrive in our life and work.

O DEATH, WHERE IS THY STING?

In comic drawings, death is often portrayed as a black shadow, the grim reaper, a symbol of fear. Death is thought of as evil and unholy. No wonder people are afraid of it. What would happen if we thought of death as the sunshine of new possibilities, the celebration of a consummation with eternity? I remember once hearing these words of wisdom: "Men laugh with joy when a child is born, while the child cries alone in grief. Men weep in sorrow when their loved ones die, while the dead one rejoices alone." The power of death not only serves those who have gone before us, it is also there to serve the living who take the requisite time to contemplate the lessons contained in its mystery.

Before you can be truly free to live, you must be free to confront your deepest fears that hold you back from striving for your highest aims. Looking death straight in the eye, you will come to conquer life's last great obstacle.

GIVE UP SURVIVAL, KNOW THE ECSTASY OF THRIVING

Because you are in fear of not surviving, you work hard trying to live a disciplined life of self-imposed deprivation. You do your duty, work at getting ahead, attempt to bring glory to yourself and your family. In fact, deprivation derived from the instinct of survival is no virtue. Life never means to deprive you. Living well means living a life of fulfilling your righteous fantasies.

Marie is a fifty-three-year-old professional woman who immigrated from France to the United States thirty years ago. Recently, she was offered a rent-free house in France for two months if she could afford the time away from her work. Although she had visited the country from time to time for business conferences, she longed to have the opportunity to repatriate for a while to the land of her youth and childhood. But the high cost of hotel rooms had always prohibited her from staying longer than a week for each of her past visits.

Now, facing an opportunity to fulfill her greatest fantasy, she hesitated. She thought about her already

overstretched workload and the projects she was supposed to have initiated over the past year that she had
been putting off because of lack of time. There was
no way she could spare two months for leisure. In
her mind, there was a tug-of-war pulling between
her reality and her fantasy, survival and living.

"If I go to France," she thought, "I can fulfill my
fantasy. If I stay home, I can progress in my work."

Marie imagined the fun she could have in France—
the food, the wine, the music, the smell of the air, and
the joy of speaking French every day. The conflict in
her heart was that she had always placed her career
before everything else. Now she desperately tried to
find a "legitimate" reason to go. She thought of the
possibility of visiting some potential business partners,
but she could not justify to herself that she needed two
months for that. Finally, she decided to erase from her
mind the idea of going to France—she could not afford two months of her time just to fulfill fantasies.

When she shared her decision with a friend, the
friend gave this advice: "You weren't born to work
yourself to death. You were born to fulfill your desire
for experiences. To live well, which includes fulfilling
your righteous fantasies, leads you to complete your

desire to experience life. To your soul, the fulfilling of fantasies is as important as accomplishing your career goals. It is wrong to die without satisfying those fantasies." The light clicked on for Marie. She packed her bags and went.

I met Marie recently in France. She told me that miraculously during her stay in France she ran into her old high school lover, whose wife had just passed away. Now they are married, and her job was moved to France permanently by her American company.

Life never meant to deprive us of having fun; rather, our fear of survival puts us on an endless treadmill of monotonous existence. Give up the desire to survive, so you can know the ecstasy of thriving.

CONCLUSION

When you are willing to not survive, the static of uneasiness flees while harmony and calmness set in. Without mastering this state, your emotions are a pendulum flying between the fear of failure and the desire for victory.

The Rainmaker has to not care about whether he

is able to bring rain or not. Nor can the Rainmaker care about his professional reputation. Thoughts such as whether he will have to give the money back, or if his wife will leave him, can never enter his mind. The Rainmaker knows life has ways of always taking care of itself, including whether the village will ever see rain again. He focuses on bringing harmony into himself and lets the heavens bring the rain. He is at peace within himself and the world. Giving up survival will put your mind at ease, and without much effort, positive results will begin to surface miraculously.

GRANT
YOURSELF
GRACE

We all pray at one time or another for Grace to give us an easy life and have good fortune smile upon us. We also try to get into the good graces of people who have the power to influence others and grant us favors. When we fall from grace with the "powerful" and "influential," we feel unworthy and devastated by their disapproval. However, have you ever considered granting yourself the grace of your own mind? The *only* reality that exists for you is in your own mind. When your mind showers its grace upon you, the whole world opens up.

An agitated mind is like an out-of-tune radio— powerless to receive or broadcast messages. As long as our mind is agitated, we are out of communication with the universal energy. Putting the mind at ease seems like a good idea and a simple principle; however, it is easier said than done. In order for the mind to release the deathlike grip it uses to hold our lives in place, the mind must feel the freedom to let go. But merely telling the mind to relax and trust in the universal power will not bring it to relaxation because, for most of us mortals, it is difficult to instantly purge the mind of its inherent panic. What the mind needs is illuminating knowledge to cure it of its sense of unease.

STUCK ON THE ROLLER COASTER

When you are on a thrilling/terrifying roller coaster, whether you enjoy the ride or not, you are momentarily the hostage of the roller-coaster ride. This feeling of being helpless and frustrated is the same experience as perceiving life's overwhelming demands engulfing you. Demands such as making a decent living, providing for your family, meeting your financial obligations, getting ahead in your job, fighting another battle, winning another war—the list goes on and on. Before you know it, life is not so much fun anymore; you become the hostage of life.

Our Rainmaker knows the secret: The only way you can escape the horror of life is to take refuge in your own mind. Just as on the roller-coaster ride, the only choice you have is to choose to enjoy the ride or endure the experience. You have control of how you wish to feel about the ride, but you are not permitted to stop the ride.

Once I went on a journey in Peru to visit the Lost City of the Incas in Machu Pichu. The trip began from San Francisco, where I transferred in Los Angeles to catch Air Peru to Lima. From Lima I took a domestic flight to Cusco. The single daily flight to Cusco arrived in the early afternoon, while the only means of transportation to Machu Pichu was the train, which left at six the next morning.

I was forced to stay the night in Cusco. Cusco is located at an elevation of twelve thousand feet above sea level, and the local coca tea did nothing to ease my altitude sickness as the locals had promised. I called room service every hour on the hour throughout the night to bring me the oxygen tank—I was dying. By the time I arrived at Machu Pichu, all I wanted to do was go home. Yet, home seemed so far away with so many hurdles to be crossed again. As I was laying in my hotel bed feeling sorry for myself, I thought, "This is exactly like a roller-coaster ride. Now I'm stuck in no-man's-land."

At that instant I realized I could continue to feel bad or simply choose to enjoy the rest of the trip. In fact, with a gracious mind-set, the remainder of the trip was delightful. I learned that Inca culture was full of mystery; the temple had been built by hand with stone joints that were fitted together seamlessly without cement, some as large as five-story buildings, deep in the middle of a jungle in the Andes Mountains. It turned out to be one of my most enjoyable trips.

A great master once said, "Without the grace of your own mind, even in heaven, you will be without peace." Taking refuge in your own mind, granting yourself grace, is the means to escape the nightmare of unpredictability and fickleness of life.

STOP THE WHIPPING

Sid, an adviser to the president of a multinational bank, once said to me, "There are three sides to me:

In the first state, I am very aggressive, opinionated, and expressive. In the second state, I feel neutral and detached. In the third, I am full of self-doubt, and my mind puts me down. When I am in the last state, I feel like I'm worthless, a pure phony."

From time to time, everyone experiences unworthiness. In fact, when we compare ourselves to our Creator and to our own unlimited, inner potential, we may conclude that we have not turned out so well. However, letting your mind grab you and use your feelings of unworthiness as a lash to whip you doesn't work. Soberly acknowledging that we fall short of our true potential is affirmative evidence that everything is on target. Introspection is a healthy state of mind for personal and professional growth.

RECASTING FROM HOSTAGE TO FREE PERSON

Without the grace of your own mind, even if you are given the grace of the world, you will proceed to sabotage your positive outcome. Some film and music stars, who are thought by the rank and file of the world to have everything, end up committing suicide or overdosing on drugs. The mind can be your best friend or worst enemy—creating private heavens or hells.

When Sid, mentioned earlier, is at his low point, he regards his dynamic high points as false illusions. In fact, his high points are more reflective of his spirit nature. The issue is not what is phony or real. Instead, it is that the mind is seeking to identify with a greater force that is the core source of its dynamism. As long as Sid views his achievements as the result of his own effort, his mind will use this fallacy as a pin to puncture his ego's balloon when it is short of air and vitality.

Because his unconscious mind knows that he is part of that unique substance of the gigantic force of Creation, it is trying to reveal to him the truth, that he is not the ultimate source of his accomplishments. By practicing the awareness that your power to accomplish is derived from your Maker, you will gain the grace of your mind with every breath taken. You will see life's pace transformed from a struggle to a state of spontaneity. In life's play, you have a choice to recast yourself from a hostage to a free person.

THE ANTIDOTE FOR
AN ABUSIVE MIND

You may have the type of mind that drives you to achieve, but no matter how well you do, your mind is never satisfied. Instead of being your friend, it acts like a cruel parent. If you were brought up by abusive or even well-meaning but exacting parents, you may experience your mind acting against you just as your parents did, even if they are now absent from your life. It constantly berates you for never being good enough.

The Chinese have a five-thousand-year history of child abuse. I come from a family that for generations without exception had a history of severe child abuse, which included both emotional and physical punishment. For example, my father's stepmother, during a snowstorm one freezing winter in Manchuria, China, locked my uncle out of the house, forcing him to spend the night huddled in the snow because he came home empty-handed, unable to get credit from the shop owner. This act of cruelty caused my uncle to permanently lose his hearing.

On my mother's side of the family, it was not much better. My maternal grandmother, when hitting my

155

mother with heavy wooden blocks, would lock the door of the firewood storage room, anticipating that her neighbor might come to interfere with her unique brand of punishment. One day, concerned that my mother would be killed by my grandmother, the neighbor rode his horse for an hour into town to drag my grandfather out of the local opium den. My grandfather immediately arose from the warm, silken pad that he was occupying with his favorite concubine and rode home. Upon arriving, he broke down the storage-room door and proceeded to savagely beat my grandmother.

In five thousand years of Chinese history, there has been no concept of child abuse. Parents are always right. The Chinese say, "Beating is love, and scorn is tenderness." Under this concept, *anything* the parents can possibly do to the child is said to be for the child's own good. When the physical bruises are long gone, the scars of the emotional damage spill over into every aspect of the child's life after he or she has grown to adulthood.

Because I, their firstborn, was a girl, my parents considered themselves cursed from my first day forward. They even blamed me for the communists taking over in China and for their ensuing loss of wealth. They also blamed me for stealing my brothers' health and wisdom. (One brother was left lame from a case of childhood polio; the other, although a talented artist, is not terribly gifted with life skills and common sense.)

For years after I had left them, my mind behaved just like my parents—whipping me and putting me down. Then I found an antidote that granted me instant freedom. Now, each time my mind criticizes me, I recite, out loud or silently, an acknowledgment of the supreme truism as I have come to know it: "I am perfect and complete. I am the creation of that glorious perfection."

As I repeat this truth with great conviction, instantly I feel a lift that releases the energy of my mind's vicious power. Now, before my mind even gets to start its negative routine, I have learned to repeat this mantra, and my mind calms down. In time, the mind that had acted like a disparaging parent is transformed into a supportive friend. Now I don't have to repeat this mantra; I really see how wondrous I am. What a shame that my parents can't see it.

For some mysterious reason, we choose a certain set of parents and grow up in a particular environment that is best for our spiritual unfolding. Your ultimate parents are your Heavenly Father and Divine Mother. Whatever perfection They have, you have. The more you recognize this truth and hold yourself to be perfect, the more you will manifest your perfection.

You don't have to become the victim of your culture, your family's "well-intended" denunciations, or your own self-criticisms. You are bigger than all of your unfortunate circumstances. Be good to yourself; be sweet to yourself. Don't build a case against yourself. This perfection is living and thriving within you, as you.

DROP THE AFFIRMATIONS, ADOPT THE MANTRAS AND PRAYERS

I would like to draw a distinction here between the use of affirmations and the use of prayers and mantras. When I use the term *mantra,* I want to be clear that I am appropriating a Sanskrit word to define a universal principle, not advocating a certain religion. Whether you call it "praying without ceasing" or "practicing the presence of God," a mantra is not the exclusive right of any specific sect. In fact, although many of us like to feel that we have an edge when it comes to knowing the Maker and His methods, all of the great religions have similar techniques, forms, and truths that mysteriously have been independently sourced by their founders. So your mantra or prayer of choice should come from that particular religious discipline with which you are most comfortable.

Many of our positive-thinking lecturers, past and present, teach the technique of affirmation. Although some have achieved results with these practices, it is my contention that the tool of prayer might be better suited to most temperaments.

The major distinction is that an affirmation may be derived from any source and, because of its origin, may produce a limited or weakened result. The old "Every day, in every way, I am getting better and better" type of affirmation does not have the inherent power for some people to counteract the negative programming that has built up in their minds over a lifetime. Their minds may be self-defeating by answering the affirmation with a sarcastic "Oh, yeah?"—which leaves them spinning their psychic wheels, getting nowhere, and most definitely not getting "better and better." Mundane affirmations, being born of the earth, are subject to the dualism of the physical world, the mental polarities that cause us so many problems, pulling us in opposing directions.

Prayers or mantras, on the other hand, are of divine origin. Usually, they are a repetition of the divine name, a scriptural phrase, an honored traditional prayer, or a universal truth. Thus, being born of the divine, mantras are not subject to the dualism of the earthly laws, and they carry within their essence the seed of divine power and truth. This is the real earth-shaking power that can change lives and circumstances to move you into the dynamic power vortex that you need to manifest all of your worthy dreams for your life.

When practicing a prayer or mantra, you are not aligning with your limited mental power or success but with the divine power and truth, which can indeed move mountains.

GIVING GRACE TO OTHERS

Granting yourself grace is not easy to do, especially if you customarily hold a nasty attitude toward others.

It is impossible for your mind to be nice to you if it has been habitually cruel and vicious toward those who cross your path.

If there is any hope for your mind to grant you grace to recast you as a free person, you need to make every effort to control your hatred toward others. You may not consider yourself a hateful person, but consider whether you burn with rage when people slurp their soup, pick their nose, abort their unborn, marry a gay person, and so on. You may believe with very good reason that they deserve the mental poison darts you throw at them, but a vicious mind is always rooted in a vicious heart. As Lord Buddha said, "When I refuse to take in the abuse from the abuser, then his gift of viciousness will be returned and absorbed by the one who handed out the abuse." How hateful you are toward others will determine how hateful your mind will be to you in equal dosage.

GRANT YOURSELF WEALTH

Your mind can create heaven and hell as well as grow money on earth. Recently, an old girlfriend of mine whom I had not seen or talked with for over twenty-five years telephoned me. She said that she had gone through a great deal of trouble to connect with me. She had seen me many times on CNN, on recent interviews with Larry King, and so on. She asked numerous questions about my life to catch up.

Among the many things that I said to her was that I had just gotten back from working in China for a couple of days. She commented on how lucky I am to be able to travel around the world and get paid for it. She then asked me how much money I had received for a day's work. Because she was a childhood friend I told her. She was silent for a while. Then, with her voice shaking in anger, she said, "I cannot understand what you could possibly do that is worth that kind of money." I did not bother to answer her question because I knew she would not understand.

She demonstrated clearly one of the key reasons why she is not getting paid at such a level of compensation. When one considers that a Hong Kong starlet makes one hundred thousand U.S. dollars for an hour of poor singing, and that some Hollywood stars receive eight-figure salaries for working a couple of weeks, we see that our inherent worth is relative to and dependent on the agreement that we have generated for ourselves in the world at large. But before the world can shower us with our just rewards, we have to experience our own worthiness from within.

Money does not grow on trees—it grows in our minds. How much you should get paid is not controlled by your boss or your customers, it is controlled by you. In the depths of your own mind, where you are really honest with yourself, you have already decided how much you are worth to others. If you think you are worth fifteen dollars an hour, then you cannot get a job that pays five hundred dollars an hour because your mind is incapable of producing that mental picture.

Others perceive your worth as you broadcast your convictions through nonverbal language, emitting what you truly feel about yourself from every cell in your body. The value that you project to others through your thought processes, consciously or unconsciously, is the value that others will sense to be your true worth.

Furthermore, if you do not know your own value and do not *show* your own value to your client or boss, how can you expect them to decide how much you are worth to them? You have to be clear on exactly what kind of benefits, what kind of real value, you bring to the table.

CONCLUSION

When you are clear about the game of life, that life has no way out and you are life's hostage, you then realize only your mind can save you from the unpredictable horrors of life.

Since the human mind is a contracted version of divine consciousness, our minds contain the potential power to create positive and negative experiences and results in every aspect of our lives. Keep your mind actively attuned to the altar of divine grace as the Rainmaker did. When he first arrived in the village, he closed himself in the tent and meditated for four days, bringing divine grace back into the village. By focusing your mind on grace, your mind will gradually feel more at ease with itself so that it may more effectively do your bidding as you go about the exciting business of unfolding your destiny.

TRANSFORM THE FOUR TOXIC MOTIVATORS

Wisdom is the principal thing; therefore get wisdom: and with all thy getting, get understanding.

—Proverbs 4:7

In order to achieve the state of the Rainmaker—to work effectively with a calm mind—we must first truthfully acknowledge where we are, relative to our mental state, and how we got there. Since the beginning of mankind, primitive human emotions—desire, anger, fear, and greed—have motivated us to achieve. These four motivators have worked relatively well for millennia, causing us to take action in order to obtain our desired objectives, and more always seemed better. In modern life, survival is not as difficult, and our drives are not kept in check by external limitations like scarcity. Nonetheless, due to the fear of not having enough, we unnecessarily do more, even to the breaking point. Driven by the force of rage at not fulfilling our desires soon enough, we do even more.

THE TWO FACES OF THE FOUR TOXIC MOTIVATORS

1

DESIRE

As a dog needs a leash and a master to control its movements, desire needs sound reasoning and good judgment to provide it with proper direction. The Sufi poet Kahlil Gibran said, "Your soul is oftentimes a battlefield, upon which your reason and your judgement wage war against your passion and your appetite."

Every motivational guru teaches that the first step to success is to set goals—and there is nothing wrong with setting goals and objectives. Desire guided by wisdom, such as the desire to excel or the desire to do good for others, is beneficial to everyone. However, as long as your actions are motivated by a raw, crude desire, the remaining three toxic motivators will surely surface. When any desire is thwarted, it causes frustration, and suddenly the nobility of your desire vanishes while anger, fear, and greed take charge.

When you desire the wrong thing, even when obtaining the object of your desire, you will not be happy. Unease and aggravation will persist because no object can fix the internal flaw of unwise motivation. When your desire is proper and in line with your destiny, satisfaction and fulfillment inevitably follow. You will enjoy freedom from anger, fear, and greed.

2
ANGER

When desires are thwarted, anger sets in. A wise sage once stated, "Anger is the worst of the inner enemies because of its connection to the unending chain of useless desire. Whenever there is dissatisfaction, there is anger."

Anger may be triggered by unfulfilled desires, but

once anger sets in, good judgment flees and a temporary insanity results from the loss of conscious discrimination. When a child is denied by his mother the candy bar he has pulled from the supermarket shelf, he screams as if being beaten within an inch of his life. Because anger is such a basic and coarse human emotion, children's unpretentious behavior serves as a mirror for us more sophisticated adults. We might take a less dramatic approach to unrealized desire, but its effects can result in stress, ulcers, heart attack, or an escape into alcoholism. A salesman I knew was long anticipating the successful closing of a large transaction. When his client decided to go with another supplier, out of his anger and desperation he gave the client a heavy left and right and ended up in jail.

On the other hand, anger applied wisely for a positive purpose can be an effective tool. A tempered anger against yourself when you fall short of your best is commendable—it can cause your mind to challenge itself in reaching for the higher mark next time. Anger for setting the vision for our lives too low can open our minds to include the unthinkable and expand the horizons of our destiny. Anger to-

ward one's employees can be an effective business
tool, which may shake them from their failure hyp-
nosis and allow them to reach beyond their self-
imposed limitations. Anger about injustice motivates
us to take up social causes, thereby helping reform
the world we live in. Even Jesus Christ, upon seeing
the money changers denigrating the temple, went in
and threw a fit, overturning tables and tossing the
merchandise about.

3
FEAR

If fear arises out of reaching for misguided desires,
it uselessly disrupts our peace of mind. Fear is not located outside of ourselves in the object of our fear (as
we often forget); rather it is located within our hearts.
Fear burns away all the noble qualities of man and
robs us of our creativity, innovation, dynamism—
even our normal standard of performance.

In ancient China there was a champion archer
who had never missed a single bull's-eye. Once, he
enrolled in a national competition and missed every
shot. The people were puzzled and went to ask a
master, why so? The master said, "His fear of losing

his title, honor, and position caused his eyes to be blinded."

Conversely, the emotion of fear can be our life-saver. When we are afraid of fire, that fear protects us from getting burned. Because of fear, we do not dive into the ocean without proper training and equipment or jump out of an airplane without a parachute. Wise fear guides us in our daily lives to carefully calculate risk factors and seek out the most creative and innovative solutions. Those who never experience fear do so because they have done nothing but live a monotonous existence, never challenging themselves or expanding against their limitations.

4
Greed

Sometimes when we are fortunate enough to obtain some of our wanton desires, greed creeps in—enough is never enough. One becomes like a child feasting on his portion of the meal while his eyes are fixed on the platter of food in the middle of the table. He wants more and more, until he gets indigestion.

Adults are no different from children in this respect. Children set simple objects as the targets for their greed while adults set more elusive goals to attain. A man might have a beautiful wife and a wonderful family, and still, due to the power of greed, he becomes bewitched by the "beautiful" women that he has not yet conquered. Greed generated for the sake of indulging in harmful desires brings one to a dispiriting end. President Clinton is a good example of this with his apparent never-ending desire for more and different women. While Mr. Clinton has performed superbly as a national leader, due to his sexual greed he has jeopardized his presidency and put the White House in crisis.

But if one is greedy for wisdom, virtue, and knowledge, it results in actions that will benefit oneself as well as the world at large. President Clinton is also a prime example of one who is greedy to improve the lives of the American people and further world peace.

CONCLUSION

All emotions under Heaven have their positive and negative purposes. Like a hat and shoes, if you wear the hat on your feet and shoes on your head, then they are counterproductive. If you wear them properly, they are useful.

In the early stages of our Rainmaker's life, he too was motivated by the four toxic motivators. By understanding the dualistic nature of desire, anger, fear, and greed, he began to be watchful and examine his motives for his actions. He determined whether they were motivated out of desperation or by an affirmation for life. By this introspection he was able to turn the four toxic motivators into the four positive motivations and let them guide his life from victory to victory.

THIRD SECRET

DISCOVER THE DIVINE POWER

STOP REACTING, START RESTFULLY CONTROLLING

Imagine our Rainmaker first arriving at the village. The villagers have not seen a drop of rain for five years. Yet, during the five years, they have seen Rainmakers come and go, money spent and money wasted on the employment of Rainmakers. Hopes are raised and then dashed with each new Rainmaker's broken promises. When our Rainmaker arrives at the village, he must carefully fine-tune his mind to shield himself from reacting to the emotions of the villagers. Otherwise, he would have no hope of bringing a single ounce of harmony to himself, not to speak of the whole village.

When you drive on the freeway, you learn to react to the traffic situation. In the workplace, when people attack you, you learn to react to protect yourself. In your business dealings, at the negotiating table, you react to the cards that are dealt to you. You react to your husband's or wife's aggression. Through the instinct of survival, reacting to your environment has become second nature to you.

Reactionary people are always controlled by the person or element that imposes the impetus to action upon them. When you operate out of reaction, you lose control. You have been swept from your power center. Reacting causes you to appear to be weak. Worst of all, you *feel* weak. As long as you are reacting, you have lost sight of your own agenda.

The following methods are ways to move yourself from reacting to restfully controlling:

1

BE THE ACTOR AND THE DIRECTOR

Instead of functioning by acting and reacting, with your reaction always one step behind the person who is imposing his or her will upon you, imagine splitting yourself into two halves. One part of you becomes the actor performing the action, going through your usual ten thousand daily items, while the other part of you is the director resting inside your heart, watching your actions and the activities around you. Unlike your competitors, who are operating out of acting and reacting, you will now have the edge—a team of two at work: the one who is performing the action and the other who is witnessing and directing.

The director, sitting inside you, sees the curveball coming long before the actor does. The director then decides whether you should step to the side at the last minute and let the ball pass you by or take a head-on swing. Either way, you are not blindly reacting to the situation, which will rob you of your sense of power and jeopardize your good judgment.

2
REPLENISH YOUR POWER
AND SERENITY

To be continuously reacting to life will cause spiritual and emotional depletion. No matter how you reason with yourself that you should not be stressed or overwhelmed by life, it does not work if you are mentally and emotionally overdrawn and spiritually bankrupt. Your life energy works the same way as your bank account. In the center of your heart is a pool of serenity where power, wisdom, passion, and the zeal for life renew themselves. You cannot keep withdrawing from your pool of serenity without making periodic deposits. You need to make a deposit of the nectar of life into your spirit before you can extract from the pool of enthusiasm.

3
REDO THE SCENE

If you find that you have overreacted to a molehill-sized situation with a volcanic, explosive psychic outburst, when you calm down, do an instant replay in your mind's eye. Properly adjust your reaction, then redo the scene again with these adjustments in mind. By repeating this process over and over again, you will learn to correct your tendency to overreact.

4
REST WITHIN

Like the pendulum of a clock that has ceased its wild oscillations, there is a relaxation point in every situation where all things simply settle in comfortably. This is the point where harmony, excellence, beauty, and synchronicity abide. Practicing resting within provides you with all the benefits that you would normally derive from meditation, such as reducing your stress and calming your mind. Furthermore, practicing resting within will gradually transform your actions from a state of "reacting" to one of "restfully controlling."

When the Rainmaker disappeared into his tent for four days to put himself in harmony, he didn't just go to sleep for four days. Sleep is not a true resting point for the mind and soul. While you sleep your body tosses and turns, your mind is actively creating fantasies and nightmares. Only by finding the true resting point within will your body, mind, and spirit be truly restful.

Resting within is much simpler than most people think. It is the innate nature of our being. It is about resting in the heart. The next chapter will provide the means to find this resting point.

CONCLUSION

When you feel frustrated about life, when it does not instantaneously manifest your vision, instead of having a frantic reaction, embrace restful control. Our Rainmaker knows the secret art of restfully directing his life and his environment rather than blindly reacting to the chaos that surrounds him. By operating his life from this point of restfulness, he is able to do less and achieve more.

STAY IN
THE PRESENT

How do we know when to take action and when to rely on meditation? The answer: meditation trains you to stay in the present, allowing you to live and work more effectively. Distraction can only lead to exasperation; when we cut the cord of sensory interference we find the magnificent point of true satisfaction.

EFFECTIVE TOOLS FOR THE TWENTY-FIRST CENTURY

As life becomes more complex, surface data and simple logic are no longer sufficient as the only source of information to help us in making complex decisions.

We must go beyond the obvious, bypassing the tunnel vision of standard planning processes to find bold new solutions. Of necessity, we must reach for the new frontiers of the reality beyond the visible.

Both the Harvard Business School and the leading European business school, INSEAD (located in the suburbs of Paris), have concluded from research that the two most effective new business tools for twenty-first-century executives are *meditation* and *intuition*. The same conclusion was reached at numerous other colleges.

Mr. Claude Rameau, the dean of INSEAD (honored as the Dean of the World), told me, "We do not know how to teach meditation and intuition, so we built a large meditation hall for teachers, executives, and students to just sit quietly and contemplate resting within." However, what is the so-called new is actually ancient.

Meditation, the science of internal access, allows you to discover wisdom and information that you do not know you have. This is the state of natural knowing, commonly referred to as intuition. All the things that I do well in life I have acquired by tapping into the channels of natural knowing. The knowledge and wisdom mysteriously spring up from "nowhere."

Through meditation, you will discover a fountain of limitless creativity, the outrageous intuition that resides within you. Through meditation, you are in touch with your awesome power. All things get done easier— even projects you had no idea how to do previously, miraculously you will find you are mastering them.

TECHNIQUES

The following six techniques have been proven by the ancient teachers to allow the activity-oriented mind to rest in the calming space of the heart. I have selected these methods because of their practical nature—they fit into today's hectic lifestyle, are simple to practice, and will make a profound difference to your daily life.

Merely understanding the words of the following techniques is useless to you. To derive any benefit, you must routinely put the techniques into practice, and that is easier said than done. Like a soldier of the Revolutionary War, understanding how to load the gunpowder into the firing arm will not save your life. Only through repeated practice, until your actions move to the level of reflex and become ingrained habit, can you become ready to face life's battles and win.

1

BEING IN THE PRESENCE OF SILENCE

This is the simplest way to rest in the heart—to be in solitude and to bathe in the joy of silence. Silence is the veil of God. Take time for a long luxurious bath and lock out the chaos of the world. Take a walk in the woods. There are infinite ways you can be with silence. In the center of that silence is the seat of that inner resting point.

2

FOCUSING ON A SINGLE IDEA
OR OBJECT

When the mind is vacillating, moving from one thought to another, the mind is agitated. When the mind is absorbed on one single idea or object, the mind is at ease with itself. People who play golf know this well. When players are on the course, their focus is on that white ball. They are bewitched by that white ball. Golfers may tell their office or their wife that they play golf because it is a good opportunity for business networking when, in fact, they are addicted to the joy they experience when their mind is focused deeply on one single object. So they follow the ball to the hazard or to the treetop.

For the nongolfer, taking a hot bath will give you the same experience. Close the door; lock out all of the chaos of the world. Immerse yourself in the steaming hot water. Focus your mind on letting go and empty your mind of thoughts. We often think it is the hot water that is so enjoyable. In fact, it is the act of letting go that is the comfort source for the mind. Just imagine if, while you were inside the tub, five telephone lines were ringing, demanding your attention. Would you feel restful?

3
CONTEMPLATING OPEN SPACE

Verse 85 of the Vijnanabhairava says: "You should contemplate vast open space, such as the sky or ocean, and see them as the essence of the all-pervasive, letting that feeling dissolve within you. Through this inner expansion, you will be absorbed and see everything within the universe as the scintillating light of the divine."

This is the same as the Western idea of finding time to stop and smell flowers. It is not that smelling flowers has any special meaning. Rather, when you are performing the act of smelling the flowers, you are experiencing the essence of creation, which expresses itself as the fragrance. You then have the opportunity to let the scent dissolve within you. As it touches you within, you expand inwardly and experience the whole universe as the divine creation of our Maker. Your inner vision opens up to reveal that all things in creation are bathing in the eternal light of the Divine.

The experience derived from looking into vast open spaces cradles your restless senses by the calming wellspring of the heart. This is a natural meditation. No wonder people are willing to pay premium prices for real estate with an ocean or mountain view.

4
BASTRIKA—THE BREATHING EXERCISE

Breathing is closely connected to the well-being of the mind (not to mention the life of the body). When you regulate your breath, you eradicate agitation from your mind. The reason that most ordinary human beings function from a space of reacting instead of controlling, regardless of their social position, is that the agitation of the mind prevents it from going within to rest.

This rapid breathing exercise is known as *bastrika* in Sanskrit. When one is practicing *bastrika,* he or she may appear to be having a hyperventilation attack. Yet, the mystery contained therein is way beyond the scene that meets the eye.

1
WHERE

You can do this exercise anywhere, in the midst of chaos or serenity.

2
WHEN

Whenever you feel stressful, restless, or fearful or if you just want to focus your mind and your spirit. You can practice this exercise before an important meeting or presentation. When you become very skillful at this, you can even do it in the middle of a meeting, and no one will notice.

3

How

Sit on a straight-backed chair that can comfortably support you, or sit on the floor in a cross-legged position. When you get good at this, you can even do it while you are standing or lying down. (I caution you against doing it while driving or operating machinery, since the results can sometimes be exhilarating enough to cause the sensation of dizziness.)

- Take a deep breath and let the breath flow into the bottom of your stomach while you focus your attention on the space between your navel and your pubic bone.

- Exhale completely, then *rapidly* inhale and exhale twelve times through your nose, drawing your breath into the lower part of your stomach. This will cause your stomach to rise and fall like a bellows—breathe in, breathe out, breathe in, breathe out. The only part of your body that is moving is your stomach. Your shoulders remain still.

- A set of *bastrika* consists of ten to twelve rapid breaths. This can be modified to a greater or lesser count to a set, depending on the practitioner. You can do as many sets as you want. In general, four or five sets are sufficient.

- Don't try to control your breath. The objective is to let your breath express itself freely. You may find that your exhalation is very forceful and long. You may find that, instead of you breathing, your breath is breathing itself. That is, your breathing has become involuntary. I do not mean out of control; rather, your mind is not currently directing your breath —it is directing itself. When you feel that you have had enough, your mind will have the power to stop at any time.

- Doing this breathing exercise will also provide you with instant rejuvenation. This is a great exercise to pick up your energy during the day. This is also a great exercise to prepare you for entering into a deep meditation.

5. THE <u>HAM'SA</u> TECHNIQUE

The holy men of all religions have practiced the art of breathing and breath regulation and, through these sacred techniques, have reached into the depths of their souls and the center of their hearts. In ancient times, the secret of this technique was well guarded. Students had to clean cowsheds for eighteen years to prove their worthiness to receive this profound teaching.

In Book Two of the Essene Gospel of Peace, Jesus said: "We worship the Holy Breath, which is placed higher than all the other things created. For lo, the eternal and sovereign luminous space, where rule the unnumbered stars, is the air we breathe in and the air we breathe out. And in the moment betwixt the breathing in and breathing out is hidden all the mysteries of the Infinite Garden."

Verse 24 of the Vijnanabhairava says something very similar: "The exhalation goes out, and the inhalation goes in. By steady fixation of the mind at the two spaces between the breaths, one may experience the full nature of *Bhairava*—God."

The following are the steps of this ancient meditation technique. However, even if you don't follow the steps and just sit for a while and watch your breath, all will be well.

- Select a serene place in your home, preferably a room dedicated to prayer and meditation. If that's not possible, assign a corner to be used for this purpose only. You should have a regular place for meditation, for this will help you to quickly enter into the state as you will subconsciously associate it with your practice.

- Wear loose clothing of natural fabrics—silk is preferred. In the East, silk is understood to be a enhancer of spiritual energy. If you are not ready to accept such a notion, you will at least find it extremely soothing and therefore a good choice for meditation.

- A candle or fragrance can also be used to create a serene mood. It is advisable to select the same fragrance each time, so you associate the fragrance with your meditation.

- Sit quietly on a wool mat or on a chair covered with a wool mat, with your back relaxed but erect. Again in the East it is understood that the use of wool insulates you from the distraction of the earth energy. For others, the ritual of it helps set the mood.

- Close your eyes. Bring your attention to your breath.

- Watch your breath naturally go in and out of your body.

- Listen to the sound of your breath. As you breathe in, your breath makes the natural sound of *ham,* and as you breathe out, it makes the sound of *sa. Ham* in Sanskrit means "I am"; *Sa* means "That"—Spirit. Humans breathe 21,600 times a day, and each time the breath repeats *Ham'sa,* trying to remind us of our divine heritage. "I am That" which created me. You may think the syllables as you breathe without uttering them out loud.

- Listen to your breath silently as you breathe in and out, watching the space between the inhalation and exhalation. Observe the space where inhalation meets exhalation. Behold the space between the breaths, for it is the gate to the mystery of this Universe and beyond.

- Sit for five minutes to half an hour or longer, as you see fit.

6
THE NONMEDITATOR'S MEDITATION

The experience of resting within is also available to the nonmeditator because, in a broad sense, life is one continuous meditation process. The beatific experiences gleaned from meditation are also available in our daily lives. The soldier in the midst of battle knows that, even while experiencing acute fear, he feels sometimes an exhilaration at the same time—an overwhelming experience of being alive fills him while in the very jaws of death. While looking into the eyes of fear, the soldier sees the Divine's primal power. The same may occur after a fit of rage. Our minds can become unusually tranquil because within the center of such strong emotions lies the raw, potent power of the universe.

However, it is simply easier and more dependable to consciously and steadfastly travel through this wondrous territory using the directed means of prayer and meditation than to occasionally hit upon spontaneous transcendental experiences.

CONCLUSION

Our Rainmaker has the unique ability to rest within himself so deeply that he can bring grace to the village out of sync with the Divine. He is a regular, committed practitioner of meditation. As the Chinese saying goes: "If you don't engage in meditation daily, when you are in need of the Buddha's help and attempt to grab onto the Buddha's feet, it won't work."

EPILOGUE—
LET GO

By incorporating these three secrets of the Rain-maker—fine-tuning your actions, putting your mind at ease, and tapping into the Divine power—you will enhance your ability to make the events and results in your life happen perfectly and with perfect timing. Your daily actions will become streamlined and sim-plified. Your performance will reach new peaks. There is an even more important benefit: like our Rainmaker, you will increase your ability to tap into the law of synchronicity and hidden coherence.

Auspicious persons, events, and elements—at just the right time—will come together to aid you in achieving your desired outcome. When we have pre-pared ourselves by proper alignment with the universal forces, synchronicity happens simply because it happens. Synchronicity and hidden coherence are what most of us call "good luck" because they are extraneous events that occur without being caused by any obvious, outward reason.

Since there is no specific formula to precipitate synchronicity and hidden coherence for our benefit, we have only to create the correct environment that attracts miracles into your life with perfect timing. You cannot force or orchestrate this—you can only practice the laws that generate the spiritual magnetism that draws these favorable forces. By practicing and embodying the three secrets, you will enhance your opportunity to have the law of synchronicity and the power of hidden coherence become a standard occurrence in your life.

LET GO BY LETTING GO

Through our human evolution, most of us have formed a belief system that states: "In order to be successful in my work, my life must be painful and filled with struggle." We subconsciously feel that if we do not experience the pain of effort along the way, we will not achieve our goals.

A couple of days ago, I received a letter from a friend who told me of the struggle in his life. He wrote, "I know my fear of letting go of my effort and struggle is what keeps the struggle and effort in place. Somehow, in my mind, I think letting go of effort and struggle would make my investment of years of tears and my entire existence seem like a waste. My mind feels that if I can be successful without the effort and struggle, it would mean that someone or something else has been in control of my life all along. My ego hates that. I also feel a layer of new fear surfacing, in that if I give up my effort and struggle, God will punish me for not struggling and trying harder."

Our mind is like a computer disk full of ingrained traces. These traces are called *samskaras* in Sanskrit— karmic impressions. In the West, we refer to them as negative programming. The *samskaras* include the billions of impressions gathered from lifetimes before. For those who do not believe that they have ever lived before, the *samskaras* would be the impressions accumulated in this lifetime or inherited through genetic memory.

The more we dwell on the same themes, the more we reinforce our behavior. The way to let go is to let go. To know the truth of a given situation is to no longer have the need to be run by the falsehood that is its opposite. Freedom is born out of experiencing that there is no need for the suffering and struggle. It is knowing, "I am releasing and letting go."

MAKE THE SHEPHERD YOUR CHAMPION

The Rainmaker's secrets elevate us from ordinary material consciousness into an extraordinary state where insights unfold with ease; we see how the spiritual elements affect our practical day-to-day world.

All my life, I have been a fierce fighter. I have always had to claw my way through to gain anything I wanted. Once, during my meditation, a vision came to me. The Good Shepherd came to me, and I was His sheep. Sheep do not have to struggle if they are willing to surrender unto the care of the Good Shepherd.

In a dream, I experienced that shepherd as my

Knight-Protector. He told me that, as the Ultimate Warrior, He should fight my battles, for He is much better at this than I. When I came out of these meditations, I could not stop crying tears of joy and relief.

Life *is* truly meant to be easy.

ABOUT
CHIN-NING

Born in Tienjin, China, Chin-Ning fled with her family to Taiwan when she was three. At the age of ten, her primary life ambition was to be a saint. In high school, she became a novice at a Catholic convent until her family decided marriage into a family of wealth and status would be a better career path for her.

In college, while still a full-time student struggling for money, she worked for a time as a television soap opera actress for the single station serving all of Taiwan, and then as a marketing representative for one Taiwanese and two European pharmaceutical companies. Being a natural-born entrepreneur with great sales ability, she caused a back-ordering for three months on a brand of cough syrup she pitched to her doctor clients and hospitals. Her earnings at the time were triple that of her professors.

Upon finishing college, she moved to America and has made the United States her home ever since. Today, she is the chairperson of the Strategic Learning Institute, the president of Asian Marketing Consultants, Inc., the founder of the non-profit organization WomanWorldWide, and the most successful American author in Asia, where her books have outsold those of authors such as Stephen Covey, Tony Robbins, and Tom Peters. Her books, *Thick Face Black Heart* and *The Asian Mind Game,* have reached the top of best-seller lists in Australia, Malaysia, Singapore, Indonesia, Taiwan, and China.

Through books, speeches, seminars, and tapes, Chin-Ning has touched millions of lives in over forty countries. She is highly revered among notable policy makers, corporate executives, foreign dignitaries, theologians, professors, and entrepreneurs. She has received more than ten thousand letters from around the world in which readers have shared their experiences of dramatic life transformations precipitated by her writings.

Chin-Ning's work is highly praised by the international media, including CNN, *USA Today,* the *Financial Times, People's Daily* in China, and the Asia editions of *People, Bazaar,* and *Vogue,* to name a few. She counts a number of prestigious multinational corporations among her clients, who refer to her as "The Bridge to the Pacific Century" and "The Strategist." During the 1996 Democratic presidential convention, she was honored as Woman of the Year by the international organization Women of the World.

A most extraordinary thinker, Chin-Ning presents the warrior philosophy of Asia as the premier vehicle for mastering strategic thinking in the corporate world as well as in daily life. She fuses timeless wisdom and spirituality with practical business tactics for solving life's ever-changing challenges.

Dear Reader:

If you wish to be on Chin-Ning Chu's mailing list to receive more information on other products or seminars by Chin-Ning, please mail or fax the following information:

Name: _____

Company: _____

Title: _____

Address: _____

State: _____

Postal code: _____

Country: _____

Telephone: _____

Fax: _____

E-mail address: _____

☐ Please contact me regarding having Chin-Ning as the keynote speaker for my company or association's function.

You may contact us at:
   Strategic Learning Institute
   PO Box 2986
   Antioch, CA 94531 [USA]
   Tel: (925) 777–1888; Fax: (925) 777–1238
   E-mail address: cnc@strategic.org
   Websites: www.strategic.org
            www.chinningchu.com